The Fragility of Concern
for Others

Contemporary Continental Ethics
Series editors: Bryan Lueck, Southern Illinois University
Edwardsville and Lucian Stone, University of North Dakota

Normative Ethics from a Continental Perspective

The books in this series address pressing and difficult ethical questions
from the perspective of Continental philosophy. They offer new ways
of thinking about moral phenomena and raise challenging questions
that have not been considered before. The series includes work in the
field of normative ethics, both theoretical and applied. Space is also
given to treatments of social, political and aesthetic questions that
intersect with ethical considerations.

Editorial Advisory Board
Andrew Benjamin, Alphonso Lingis, Ladelle McWhorter, Eduardo
Mendieta, Ann V. Murphy, Kelly Oliver, Danielle Petherbridge,
Anthony Steinbock

Books available
Obligation and the Fact of Sense
Bryan Lueck
The Responsibility to Understand: Hermeneutical Contours of Ethical Life
Theodore George
The Fragility of Concern for Others: Adorno and the Ethics of Care
Estelle Ferrarese, translated by Steven Corcoran

Visit our website at: edinburghuniversitypress.com/series/epcce

The Fragility of Concern for Others

Adorno and the Ethics of Care

Estelle Ferrarese
Translated by Steven Corcoran

EDINBURGH
University Press

Edinburgh University Press is one of the leading university presses in the UK. We publish academic books and journals in our selected subject areas across the humanities and social sciences, combining cutting-edge scholarship with high editorial and production values to produce academic works of lasting importance. For more information visit our website: edinburghuniversitypress.com

Edinburgh University Press Ltd
The Tun – Holyrood Road
12(2f) Jackson's Entry
Edinburgh EH8 8PJ

First published in hardback by Edinburgh University Press 2021

Typeset in 10/13 Meridien by
IDSUK (DataConnection) Ltd

A CIP record for this book is available from the British Library

ISBN 978 1 4744 6739 1 (hardback)
ISBN 978 1 4744 6740 7 (paperback)
ISBN 978 1 4744 6741 4 (webready PDF)
ISBN 978 1 4744 6742 1 (epub)

Contents

It is almost as if philosophy – and most of all the great, deep, constructive philosophy – obeyed a single impulse: to get away from the place of carrion, stench and putrefaction.

Theodor W. Adorno, *Metaphysics: Concept and Problems* (1965), p. 117

Introduction

To rearm critical theory through feminism – such is the purpose of this book. It takes up a reflection on the social conditions of caring, or having concern, for others, and defends a conception of morality that is materialist and political – always-already political. But what animates it and provides the reason for its existence is a project to renew and sharpen critical theory through feminism. This book thus does not intend simply to correct or supplement critical theory, to reveal a blind spot in it or emend its shortcomings concerning gender, both historical and current – odd as it may be, critical theory can be said to be feminist only at the margins of its German empire, thanks notably to the works of Nancy Fraser and Jessica Benjamin. On the contrary, the principle that this book sets out from is that feminism has something to say about moral philosophy, capitalism and processes of moral subjectification *in general*. It refuses to give up the general just because we have been driven from it (and yet grasps it precisely in its tension with the particular). It holds fast to the conviction that feminism can and must shape the critical act, whether this latter is brought to bear on patriarchy and male domination or not.

Critical theory is today absorbed in an exercise of methodical justification. Obsessively, it searches for a set of foundations that could be organised in monist fashion around a concept (for example, for Habermas and for Honneth all social phenomena must be adequately understood and criticised through the prism of communicative action or recognition, respectively). And it tends towards describing and denouncing the pathologies of a morally saturated social whole, as we see in Honneth's return to Hegel's philosophy to seek in it a (potentially) moral dimension of the market and a philosophy of history bearing moral progress, or in Rahel Jaeggi's ethical functionalism, which unfolds the way in which forms of life evolve by setting out to solve problems of an ethical order.

In this work, we return to a more conflicting, broken version of critical theory, that of Theodor W. Adorno, frequently described as aporetic for this very reason. Built on unruly borrowings, and willingly fragmentary, Adorno's critical theory arises from a dialectic that is not a reconciling pendulum movement, and from a minimal, negative and negativist morality. Adorno's frequent stating of unresolved contradictions, his declaration of the impossibility of formulating a grand morality, has led many to the conclusion that he does not pass philosophical muster.

Yet Adorno's work still enjoys the aura of great German philosophy, which radically distinguishes it from the discourse of theorists[1] of care, my other theoretical resource here, which, being feminist, often resting on disciplinary uncertainties, invariably taking the pathetic and the soiled as its objects, is a priori inaudible. Discussing the particular in argument with Hegel, even when taking byways, as Adorno does in *Negative Dialectics*, is not the same as approaching it from the body of a bedridden old man.

These theoretical corpuses can nonetheless be brought closer together through their many shared thematic motifs and epistemological commitments, which I examine in the first chapter. The most salient theme is undoubtedly that of vulnerability. Its density in Adorno's work is exceptional. Though the word itself crops up rarely, 'vulnerability' comprises all that falls under the many evocations of mutilated lives within the administered world, of individualities and collectives damaged by instrumental rationality and power. Theories of care put forward a perspective that, unlike in Adorno's philosophy, arises immediately as an ethics, and sets out from an intricately supported anthropology of vulnerability and dependence. It focuses attention on the awareness of one's ability to inflict wrong on others and on the notion of responsibility – as opposed to those of duty and equity – which implies the ability to perceive and respond to a need or to suffering.

Above all, however – and this is the hypothesis underlying this essay – both Adorno's critical theory and theories of care are threaded by a common theme that distinguishes them from other theories of vulnerability: the vulnerability they explore is one that is specific to the moral agent, to the caregiver exposed to political and social mechanisms, or bound to forms of life likely to prevent her from perceiving needs or suffering, to hold her back from responding to them, or to induce her to respond to them inappropriately. This vulnerability is defined by the ever-present threat that socio-political forces may neutralise the conditions of morality.

Joan Tronto identifies the lack of ability to perceive and respond to a need as a 'form of evil' that she calls ignorance.[2] Adorno speaks of 'coldness', which he often qualifies as 'bourgeois', as the ability not to be affected by the distress of others through distancing oneself and acting as spectator. Such is what made Auschwitz possible.[3] Both theories are interested in the social production of this ignorance, this coldness. This is what I call the fragility of concern for others.

In endeavouring to understand it, I seek to avoid two pitfalls. The first is the naturalisation of this care or concern, towards which society would then merely constitute an external threat. The second is the identification of moral acts inserted in material, institutional arrangements and relations of force and domination with a morality that is contaminated in its normative content, or even nowhere to be found.

Taking Adorno's social philosophy as a point of departure and submitting it to questioning by way of some ideas defended by theories of care, I am able to keep these two counter-models at a distance and attempt instead to think through the *social* fragility of the concern for others in its force, the moral act to which it enjoins us and its political stakes.

The very conducting of this study ought not lead us to imagine that theories of care are being attributed any exaggerated unity; indeed, their presuppositions about the texture of moral dispositions, or even the content of the word 'care' itself, vary greatly, ranging from Carol Gilligan's more or less explicitly stated essentialism to Joan Tronto's highly political conception of the social distribution of responsibilities. It is from the angle of their sensitivity to the social conditions of a moral judgement and a moral act that I tackle them as a unified corpus.

Moreover, if this exercise involves a feminist critique of Adorno's theory of moral dispositions, my aim is not to engage in an overarching examination of Adorno's (fragmentary) moral philosophy from the standpoint of gender relations, a philosophy that, as we know, gathers meditations on the themes of freedom, on the relationship between relativism and nihilism, and even on the nature of reason. My aim is rather to highlight a blind spot in his analysis of the fragility of attention to others, and to reflect on the theoretical, moral and political consequences of differentiating between the social mechanisms that order the moral dispositions of men and women in capitalist societies, or at least in some of them, which I gather under the expression 'concern for others'.

With this expression, I aim to forge a category broad enough to accommodate diverse dispositions and affects, provided that they overlap with an attention to the needs and sufferings of others that is coupled with a felt injunction to respond to them, regardless of the names given and the forms favoured by the theoretical currents that have considered them in history: care, solicitude, sympathy, compassion, benevolence, mercy and so on.

The first movement of our philosophical inquiry into the fragility of concern for others involves extracting from Adorno's work and from care theories the theoretical constellations at the centre of which this concern is central (Chapter 1). This movement then allows us, in a second step, to compare the causalities and contours respectively attributed by Adorno and by care theorists to the threats that hover over a concern for others. The ensuing conversation reveals the blind spot of the Adornian approach: the fact that the distribution of moral dispositions is differentiated according to gender. Conclusions may then be drawn from this distribution in terms of a critical theory of contemporary capitalism. Our form of life, tense with generalised indifference, nevertheless produces a compartmentalised attention to others, one limited to very specific tasks and fields and assigned to women (Chapters 2 and 3). The third part of the study consists in thinking about these fulgurant moral acts, which nevertheless testify, however fleetingly, to a real concern for others; at issue is, on the one hand, to grasp the fragility inherent in *enacting* such concern and, on the other hand, to determine the validity these gestures can claim in a world transfixed by unaffection. In particular, how can we apprehend the moral content of an enacted concern that turns out to be the product of a gendered distribution of moral dispositions, this latter being a condition of possibility for the capitalist market (Chapter 4)?

1 Confluences

The thematic foundation constituted by a reflection on the fragility of concern for others would perhaps be sufficient to authorise staging a dialogue between Adorno's philosophy and ethical theories of care. The ethical and political consequences drawn from this fragility on both sides can, however, be reconciled in at least four further aspects: the place given to the body in the conception of morality; the attention given to the individual as threatened by the general and the universal; an approach to moral reasoning out of keeping with philosophical tradition; and the postulate of a continuity between internal and external nature and the moral obligations that flow from this nature. These confluences are backdropped by irreducible discrepancies on the social and political level.

A Body-Centred Morality

Both theoretical corpuses give a prominent place to the body. Adorno not only calls for a show of 'solidarity' with the bodies of others, with their flesh exposed to suffering and torture, but he conceives this solidarity as arising from an aversion to physical suffering, as a movement of disgust when faced with it or its possibility; that is as having a physical substrate. He thus gives a particular twist to a theoretical move that is more broadly characteristic of the Frankfurt School.

The first generation of critical theorists understand the fundamental fragility and passivity of the human body, and even of the animal body, as a fundamental medium of knowledge and politics. Critical thinking must be built against suffering; to establish the diagnosis of an era and its pathologies, suffering has to be brought to light. For critical theory the apprehension of suffering is a *condition* of true knowledge. At the turn of the 1940s, Horkheimer posited that critical consciousness could no longer be conceived of as knowledge of the laws of history but as an experience of suffering, including animal suffering; similarly, in *Negative Dialectics*, Adorno maintained that, 'The need to lend a voice to suffering is a condition of all truth. For suffering is objectivity that weighs upon the subject; its most subjective experience, its expression, is objectively conveyed.'[1]

In this first version of critical theory, it would no doubt be inapposite to speak of a simple 'attention' to suffering and far more accurate to speak of concern. Why? Because it is considered problematic to adopt the stance of someone who explains, since by explaining the harm suffered one is spared from taking the full measure of it:

There are people who will not be disturbed about the existence of evil because they have a theory that accounts for it. Here, I am also thinking of some Marxists who, in the face of wretchedness, quickly proceed to show why it exists. Even comprehension can be too quick.[2]

There are traces of this position even in Herbert Marcuse, who states in his 1938 article 'On Hedonism' that conceiving of an emancipated society, one which removes the principle of renouncing happiness as the basis of its organisation, implies as one of its adopted aims to negate the physical suffering of the least of its members.[3]

Further, it is this epistemological status from which suffering derives its political status, because it urges social transformation: 'The physical moment tells our knowledge that suffering ought not to be, that things should be different.'[4]

We ought to note the lack of any distinction between the notions of suffering and pain in Adorno, which are deliberately rendered indivisible by the incessant switching of uses of the words *Leiden* and *Schmerz*. Accordingly, he strives to lend an intrinsically bodily dimension to any feeling of injustice or awareness of the indecency of the world as it is. Suffering of a moral or psychological type caused by oppression, alienation or wrong living seems, in Adorno's writings, either to generate physical pain very concretely or to be modelled on it, in the mode of the sensible.

In his late moral philosophy, Adorno lends the theme of bodily suffering even greater trenchancy by conceiving of one's moral bearing from a context in which the human body has been and is tortured, that is in the wake of Auschwitz, which he sees as forming the fatal outcome of modernity, of the expansion of reason and of the growing domination of nature. The body as 'torturable',[5] an expression he borrows from Bertolt Brecht, is at the heart of his reasoning about what morality can still be today. It is deployed out of the concern to refrain from, and avert, the inflicting of pain.

For Adorno, such solidarity with the tormented body of others must further be understood as 'a physical impulse'. Adorno's critical materialism, which assumes that to know something one must be touched by it, makes 'bodily feeling'[6] the only possible motivation for resistance to the production of a new Auschwitz: 'It is in the unvarnished materialistic motive only that morality survives.'[7] The history of the West has defeated all other possible moral authorities; driving them into vacuity one after the other, it therefore makes the body, as far as it is capable of disgust, the final resort for a life lived less wrongly.

In Adorno, then, the will has a somatic element. This proposition must be understood as a rejection of the idea, commonplace in the philosophical tradition, that will is composed of consciousness alone. For alongside consciousness, there is a remnant, or as he calls it a 'supplement' (*Hinzutrende*), that is an impulse illustrated in an 'abhorrence of the unbearable physical agony to which individuals are exposed even with individuality about to vanish as a form of mental reflection'.[8] The proposition is a radical one. As Christoph Menke has pointed out, this impulse cannot be reduced to what rational morality would call a 'motive'. Adorno does not speak of an impulse *to follow* this or that moral proposition, he rather explores moral propositions themselves *as* impulses. They express a moral knowledge that arises in response to the perception of an event. Moral knowledge is in itself an 'emotion'.[9]

The moral impulse, described as 'preceding the ego',[10] is therefore both extra- and intra-mental, and holds together knowledge and action. However, it is necessary that the 'suffering' felt in the face of the pain of others be taken up by consciousness and transposed into a decision, a movement that must not be understood either in terms of purification or those of sublimation of a raw material. The decision then produces a 'jolt'[11] in the causal chain of the world; it manifests a form of freedom. Adorno's materialism thus extends to his conception of freedom, the place of which is the body: 'with impulse freedom extends to the realm of experience'. [12]

This reasoning is based on a critique of Kant, whose categorical imperative rests upon identifying freedom and reason, an identification that dismisses everything outside it to the realm of constraint. Any rule I give myself that does not derive from my own reason alone is a restriction of the principle of freedom. Such a rule binds me, attaches me to something that is not myself.[13] The entire domain of impulses and interests is then cast into the realm of that on which I cannot make myself dependent. Any action carried out by virtue of an inclination is considered heteronomous and as such excluded a priori from the field of moral gestures. Adorno considers that what leads to true freedom is, by contrast, an encounter with our physical impulses, and not their subjection.

It should be noted, finally, that the place that Adorno gives to solidarity with others in their suffering when defining the moral gesture is a way of limiting the normative space conferred on the mechanism of identification. Indeed, parallel to the moral gesture, he developed a reflection on distance as a necessary response to the alienated forms of interpersonal communication and to the constitution of the masses through politically perverse processes of identification. It is, he argues, only by recognising what distances us from those who are closest to us that we can appease alterity. On the other hand, 'Wherever immediateness posits and entrenches itself, the bad mediateness of society is insidiously asserted.'[14] A sudden fit of disgust felt at the torture inflicted on another body does not presume identifying with a self that resembles me. It is not based on any role-taking or one's being guided by the reasons of another, nor does it evoke them. It simply brings two bodies together. It is an unintentional moment of consciousness and its biological past, and as such is an echo of objectivity in the subject; objectivity is thus ushered in, thanks to a pressure exerted on the body, through the impulses and conscience of the subject.

In theories of care, too, the moral gesture originates in bodily mechanisms, in that care for others is underpinned, supported and manifested by emotions and affects such as solicitude. According to theorists of care, our emotions are, as in the Aristotelian tradition, the vectors of a knowledge of the situation that the moral gesture cannot do without. They inform us about *what matters* in a given situation. What matters should not, from the perspective of an ethic of care, be seen as the result of preferences or values, but as the effect of commitments lived in the social world, which our emotions accompany and guide. They are seen 'as an aspect of composite conduct, mixing perception and reasoning on the particularities of situations, an active response to their salient features, expressing in act a hierarchy of priorities for action; and not as the "emotional", i.e. irrational, motives for rational action'.[15] They also demonstrate the importance of the ties that bind us to others, as contradictory and conflicting as these ties may be. They force us to see the world differently, confronting us with expectations, betraying disappointments about them, allowing for viewpoints on what is happening that differ from those that might be foreseeable.[16]

This approach to emotions is accompanied by a critique of the dichotomies that frequently surround representations of affects: emotion/reason, subjective/objective, passive/active, feminine/masculine. It presupposes that the boundaries between these categories cannot be sustained and denounces their ideological mobilisation and articulation with categorisations in terms of gender, class, race. Indeed, women, children, the poor and ethnic groups are frequently assigned minority status in the name of their emotional 'nature'.

There are certainly some emotions, such as envy, shame and repulsion, that present powerful barriers to observing the world from the point of view of others. However, other affects, in particular solicitude, love, compassion, respect and concern, delineate a specific – moral – orientation towards others and the relationships we develop with them.

Nel Noddings has defended one of the most radical positions on this theme, suggesting that care be considered on the model of the functioning of the mother–child dyad, the feeling that constitutes it, and the 'receptivity' it implies on the part of the mother. By receptivity, Noddings understands a way of 'feeling with', as opposed to what she considers is encompassed by the word 'empathy', which, by insisting on *understanding* others, seems to her to amount to a 'rational, Western, male' relationship with others. Receptivity, by contrast, defines an impulse; it implies refraining from analysing the expectations of others, and from treating the other as an object of knowledge; in short, it implies avoiding the analytical and objectifying mode by which consciousness imposes a structure on the world.[17] Care does not result from yielding to affects, rather it rests on a discipline of pushing back everything that threatens them or distances one from them.

More generally, care theories show that, while many analyses, sociological ones in particular, have already evoked the idea that emotions and feelings refer to a shared intelligibility or a common sense, what has not been considered is that their social significance is largely due to their manifesting a normative and moral point of view.[18] It is this blind spot that care theories set out to remedy, in particular by stressing that what is lacking in these dominant approaches to emotions is the recognition that individuals can make divergent assumptions about what situations mean, what they are supposed to feel in each case and the consequences of expressing emotions to, or in the presence of, certain others. In other words, it is in their practical, private and *particular* dimension that emotions are endowed by an ethic of care with a cognitive and moral component, and not in that they are, or ought to be, uniformly felt in a given situation.

Moreover, these theories insist on the very material and corporeal aspect of the moral gesture: care is simultaneously defined as an affect and an *activity*.[19] It is almost always an attitude, it almost always involves very concrete and frequently difficult work (especially because it involves caring for the most bodily needs of others). Pascale Molinier in particular highlights the multiplicity of ways in which the body impresses itself in the care relationship: the weary bodies of caregivers; the insistent or resistant bodies, the failing, heavy or repulsive bodies of care receivers; and the sexualised bodies of both receivers and givers.[20] A concern for others is, from the perspective of an ethic of care, a particular relationship between two (or multiple) bodies.

Care thus gets riveted to the rhythm of repetition, qua time of the body and its ever re-emerging needs. The weight given to the body in care theories entails that the moral gesture par excellence is not a unique and heroic gesture but a recommencement ever adapted, an infinite task (whether gruelling or minor).

The Particular against the General

Adorno and care theorists both take as the privileged object of moral reflection the particular in so far as it is threatened by the general.

For Adorno it is important that the particular be read each time in the light of the painful contradiction between the universal and the particular, between the system and the fragment. Adorno found compelling Walter Benjamin's view that 'the smallest cell of observed reality offsets the rest of the world',[21] and his fragmentary method, posited as a rejection of the idea, found in both Hegel and Marx, that it is through the mediation of the universal that the totality is established. He was particularly persuaded by Benjamin's idea that the historical whole can be contained in one of its parts, a part in which historical contradictions and paradoxes can be read. Adorno similarly postulates the presence of the universal in specific historical phenomena that, like Leibnizian monads, can be simultaneously both universal and particular.

The 'micrological view' adopted by Adorno, though, has nothing in common with that which uses the singular as an illustration or, conversely, as an element permitting induction: Adorno, by contrast, called for the 'banning of "examples" from the domain of dialectical method'.[22]

Knowledge really only develops when, far from setting itself the primary task of establishing the general, it attaches itself to the singular, to the individual, to the point of extricating it from its isolation. As he puts it in one of the last sentences of *Negative Dialectics*, 'the micrological view cracks the shells of what, measured by the subsuming cover concept, is helplessly isolated and explodes its identity, the delusion that it is but a specimen'.[23]

For Adorno, the empirical, social sciences are a powerful tool for forgetting the particular by crushing it under the general. According to him, social empirical research proceeds 'as if it took the idea of the social atom at its face value'.[24] Thus does it conceal a truth content despite itself: by its very methods, and the results it obtains with them, it bears witness to the fact that 'the individual is blindly subjected to the general and is itself disqualified',[25] that the general and the individual are not reconciled. Giving attention to the particular then implies refusing a threefold fetish, constituted by the sciences and a condition of possibility of the administered world: that of 'facts', that of generality and that of classification.

This is not simply an epistemological requirement, but also a question of restoring dignity to the singular, of making its own claims heard, its moral relevance. This is because the totality mutilates the particular, and this mutilation is a – and even *the* – resort of domination. The fetish of generality is a powerful mechanism of indifference to others. It allows human beings to be treated as objects, as mere elements in a series, as lives that do not count, just as the victims of the camps were. As Adorno puts it:

> this tacit assent of the primacy of the general over the particular, which constitutes not only the deception of idealism in hypostasizing concepts but also its inhumanity, that has no sooner grasped the particular than it reduces it to a through-station, and finally comes all too quickly to terms with suffering and death for the sake of a reconciliation occurring merely in reflection.[26]

A complicity thus exists between, on the one hand, Kantian morality and its categorical imperative riveted to the universal and, on the other, these mechanisms of subsumption, which organise both the mode of knowledge in contemporary society and the relationship that institutions, especially the market, have with human beings. A 'minimal morality', as Adorno attempts to outline it, must then start from the contradiction between the particular and the universal, and linger over this contradiction without trying to overcome it.

Indeed, in the opposition between universal and particular, it would be a mistake, he reminds us in his lecture series titled *Problems of Moral Philosophy*, to put all the blame on the universal and to locate all the good on the side of the particular.[27] Nor should we dwell on the singular to the point of attaching to it, or indeed, where the particular coincides with the individual, simply wall oneself inside self-preservation – or, as he puts it, 'The obstinacy of dwelling on what one merely is oneself, the narrowness and particularity of individual interest.'[28]

The task of moral philosophy is rather to think through the *contradiction* between the universal and the particular as such, to take it up as a problem, just as it pertains to the moral act to unfold between both its poles.

As regards care as a form of presence to others, it presupposes in itself a form of attention that is *differentiated*. First, in an ethic of care, ethical norms, far from being general rules to be applied, emerge within and even from networks of relation-ships.[29] The moral agent is defined by its entanglement, which is constitutive, in multiple relationships. Setting out from this thesis, an ethic of care thus marshals a conception of action as a *response*, and therefore as springing from a relationship rather than as emanating from a self. As Fabienne Brugère writes, solicitude 'comes neither from me nor from others'.[30] But then ethical norms, as products of a particular relationship, are irreproducible, non-transposable, non-generalisable. And if care originates in the world of our dependencies, it materi-alises specifically in relationships of proximity; it imposes itself on me because I am bound to *this* person, because I am *next to* this person, because she is vulnerable to *my* action or *my* inaction.

Caring for others, moreover, if it is to be caring, presupposes an attention to the needs, expressed or silent, of that person there, in their uniqueness. Attention as an appropriate atti-tude is by definition a gesture or a way of doing (or not doing) something that is adjusted to the recipient's needs, be they for distance or detachment, and is apt because it occurs at the right time. It requires sensitivity to the emotional states of the person being cared for, an experimental attitude, a 'delicate-ness',[31] or the ability to skip on to something else in specific situations. In short, it is based on an attention to the person in her singular entirety: 'it is *who she is*, and not her actions or traits subsumed under general rules' that is important in the decision taken with regard to her.[32]

As the perspective of an ethic of care considers that pro-cesses of moral and practical deliberation are inseparable, attention to the particular will only appear in gestures. Such attention does not get expressed in care in the sense that a moral context, which pre-exists in one's consciousness, is externalised or takes *shape*: it exists only in these gestures. In this vein, Pascale Molinier highlights the role played in the care provided in a retirement home by so-called small nothings: ordinary gestures whose importance comes to light when lacking, and which take effect thanks to the sensitive knowledge possessed by carers of their patients in their singularity – a gesture cannot be distinguished from the particular attention that gives it its meaning.[33]

Lending importance to the particular in this way leads to a virulent critique of theories of justice, of the many moral philosophies which, setting out from Kant, are characterised by their bias towards impartiality, and which postulate that attention to the singular is a sign of unenlightened or arbitrary reasoning. From the perspective of an ethic of care, the universal is a lure in so far as it actually represents a situated, masculine point of view. When grasping a moral problem, objectivity amounts to bringing a particularism, that of power, to the level of the universal. It is also the other name for indifference, a rhetorical tool used to confer legitimacy on a homogenising moral viewpoint grounded in abstract duty.

Both Adorno and theorists of care thus defend highly unconventional conceptions of moral reasoning, in which an emphasis is placed on the particular as the object, that is the recipient, of the moral gesture.

What Counts as Moral Reasoning

In contrast to Kantian approaches, Adorno considers that the sort of knowledge that moral deliberation mobilises is situational. On the one hand, it is not thanks to principles or ideas that a demand comes to bear on one, but rather to the situation as such, in its unbearableness. On the other hand, Adorno's moral reasoning presupposes no knowledge of the good, something that, in our – thoroughly bad – world, is impossible. He professes a negativism according to which it is possible to recognise the evil of a situation in the absence of any consistent idea of good, or even without any general knowledge of evil: 'We may not know what absolute good is or the absolute norm, we may not even know what man is or the human or humanity – but what the inhuman is we know very well indeed.'[34] The only knowledge that accompanies my action is a piecemeal knowledge, negative, immanent to the situation.

The history of care theories, by contrast, began with a book on moral psychology, Carol Gilligan's *In a Different Voice*, a work in which critical scrutiny is brought to bear on Lawrence Kohlberg's work on the stages of moral development. According to Kohlberg's Kant-inspired model, subjects reach moral maturity when they acquire an autonomous capacity for judgement and are able to decide between the interests of others and their own from an impartial position. Moral reasoning, which coincides with reasoning on justice, thus proceeds in a deductive way, setting out from universal rules and demonstrations that are applied to the particular case under consideration. Gilligan, by contrast, proposes a conception of moral judgement that presupposes the consideration of a 'contextualised' Other, not a 'generalised' one. She stresses that many feminine subjects reason within a framework formed by the moral dilemmas they are confronted with, a framework that, because it avoids any universalising procedure, can only point to a form of deficiency on the Kohlberg model; on the other hand, what becomes manifest here is a concern to maintain the relationship or even an attention to the concrete situation. Gilligan thus recasts the idea of moral judgement, in its content and form, so that it is not measured by references to general principles, but is seen as a narrative that articulates thick and specific details that take on meaning in people's life contexts.[35]

Narration, for theorists of care, figures as a process by which the moral problem and the fitting response gradually reveal themselves to the agent as she explains the surroundings of the act and the elements that shape it.[36] Refusing to consider, as theories of impartiality do, that an adequate moral judgement is one that is produced under idealised conditions, allowing for a pure exercise of thought, theorists of care admit a multitude of possible appropriate responses in any given situation; Amy, the little girl whose speech Carol Gilligan analyses so as to reveal a different moral voice, that of care, often answers 'it depends', which Gilligan interprets as marking her moral maturity. Theories of care thus present moral life as fundamentally confused: 'chaos, confusion, the intertwining of contradictory affects, the web of obscure feelings form the ordinary fabric of our moral decisions, which are sometimes barely decisions, barely vague impressions that persist, wait their time to be a little better identified and understood.'[37] Theories of justice, however, which invent original positions supposedly free from the contingencies of ordinary life, merely 'state hypotheses that freeze the ephemeral moments of ethical life', concealing the fact that 'these "freeze frames" draw upon practices that change with different contexts of moral understanding'.[38]

Theories of care, then, also accept a form of the decision's incompleteness or imperfection, which is accompanied by a certain moral discomfort with which one precisely has to 'make' do.[39]

Correlatively, both Adorno and care ethicists are severely critical of the idea of rational deliberation as preceding and justifying the moral act and they back up their criticisms with *moral* reasons.

Some care theorists, for example, thus refute arguments that seek to establish a moral distinction or indistinction between humans and animals. Any such exercise of justification assumes that the question of the moral relationship to the animal can be solved empirically, for example through making discoveries about the cognitive or affective capacities of certain species. However, our moral relationship with animals concerns our being engaged in a common world with them and thus is about always-already existing practices. The perspective that seeks to establish our community or our difference with animals on the basis of biological capacities is shown to be not only irrelevant but also unbearable from a moral point of view. All that is admissible is the *sensation* of a moral burden,[40] the repugnance felt at the sight of an injury being inflicted, on a being with whom we share a form of life.

We find a similar idea in Adorno, according to whom deliberation is, in certain situations, a gross offence in itself. Referring, in *Negative Dialectics*, to the emergence of a new categorical imperative, which is to do everything possible to ensure that Auschwitz is never repeated, he insists that this imperative is refractory to any attempt to ground it, and that examining it discursively is 'an outrage'.[41] To require or provide justification for a life that strives towards such an avoidance, which is a requirement that is *imposed* on me, is already to misunderstand the requirement in question. Such would indicate a disregard for the obligations that the *situation* brings to bear on me.

What is more, in its very claim to rationality this deliberative moment gives rise to a form of irrationality. In the ninth lecture of *Problems of Moral Philosophy*, Adorno thus raises the possible scenario of a refugee knocking on the door and asking for hospitality. Employing one's entire machinery of reflection, even though this refugee risks being killed or handed over to the police, is, according to Adorno, morally and cognitively inappropriate: 'if reason makes its entrance at this point then reason itself becomes irrational'.[42] Similarly, there are assertions such as 'do not torture' that we must not seek to justify rationally, because they would then 'fall promptly into the bad infinities of derivation and validity'.[43] As Adorno and Max Horkheimer remark in *Dialectic of Enlightenment*, there can be no rational establishment of an irrefutable argument against murder.[44]

However, just as his reflection on the contradiction between the particular and the general does not lead to the universal's elimination, Adorno's approach to moral argumentation is dialectical, far more so than that characterising the ethical theories of care. Indeed, while Adorno argues for the idea of spontaneity, defined as 'the immediate, active reaction to particular situations',[45] whose intolerable nature obliges me to act, and posits that, wherever this element of spontaneity is absent, something like a morally valid act is not possible, in the same lecture from *Problems of Moral Philosophy* he also defends the necessity of theory as follows: 'a practice that simply frees itself from the shackles of theory and rejects thought as such on the grounds of its own supposed superiority will sink to the level of activity for its own sake.'[46] A practice that renounces all theory, all reasoning, can certainly be explained by the impotence of theory in our world, Adorno admits, but by this renunciation it further increases that impotence, owing to 'the isolation and fetishization of the subjective element of historical movement, spontaneity'.[47] Therefore, there can be no question of simply dismissing a moment of abstract questioning. Rather, the philosopher must face up to a double impossibility: that of a satisfied spontaneity and that of a rational foundation for moral decisions.

For both theoretical corpuses, then, moral judgement is distinguished by its consideration of the consequences of an act or of its absence; it certainly cannot be assessed on the basis of the intention behind it.

With care theories, 'to care for' means, first, to respond *appropriately* to what and to whom we are connected. Inscribed in time, care involves a series of acts that complement or emend previous acts; it is based on a permanent attention to the needs of others in their transformation or repetitiveness, and to the effects of the care relationship on its beneficiary. Carelessness regarding the consequences of our actions, including the most everyday ones, is seen as negligence, as a morally reprehensible attitude. Nevertheless, an ethic of care is not consequentialist in that it refuses the moment of impartial calculation. As aforementioned, while such an ethics includes an injunction to partiality, it rejects the *form* of consequentialist ethics on the ground that consequentialism requires that all an action's probable effects be summed up and weighed.

Adorno's morality is sketched by taking into account not only the end and intention of my actions, but also the form of world that results from it,[48] which he does by engaging in an in-depth critique of Kantian morality and its insistence on intentions rather than consequences. For him, no act of will can be detached from all the empirical conditions under which it is arises. Moreover, it is difficult, and Adorno is inspired here as much by Friedrich Nietzsche as by psychoanalysis, to disentangle a moral intention from a shady motive, a resentment or other unconscious causes. Finally, not even the purest intention is exempt from the possibility that its realisation may result in morally unacceptable effects, which Adorno illustrates through Henrik Ibsen's play *The Wild Duck*. According to his reading of it, amidst a tangle of acts of compromise, dishonesty and betrayal, brought to light by a denunciation that is undeniably right from the point of view of intention, the plots leads to the revelation of truth that ends in the suicide of the play's only innocent character. Ibsen's work, in other words, makes it clear how one can become immoral simply by defending the moral law.[49]

This mistrust of convictions is coupled, as in care theories, with a symmetrical doubt concerning substantial and consequentialist conceptions of morality, expressed via a commentary on Hegel. To follow a model that consists in making the moral gesture coincide with the careful weighing of its effects on the world, denying or weighing the authority of the moral subject, is to make morality depend on the way of the world; such a movement conceals a form of adaptation to the existing world. Moral norms can only lose their critical edge, and the individual is still subordinated in this way to the world as it is.[50] Adorno concludes that, 'For this reason, then, there is no right life in the wrong one, for a formal ethics [based on intention, or disposition (*Gesinnung*)] cannot underwrite it, and the ethics of responsibility that surrenders to otherness cannot underwrite it either.'[51] Once again, the solution does not lie in a form of mediation, mitigation or mutual correction between two equally unsatisfactory proposals. The moral stance consists in facing the discomfort of a paradox.

Inner Nature, Outer Nature

Both theoretical corpuses are traversed by a last theme, however unevenly they develop it: that of an external nature that cannot be fully distinguished from an internal nature and that ought also to be a focus of moral attention.

In other words, Adorno and care theorists both set themselves the task of thinking through a concern for others and the natural environment, especially animal, that surrounds us. They do so not by virtue of a logic of addition – where the addition of concerns precludes incompatibility – but because the two are historically and conceptually intertwined. Human beings and nature are mutually constitutive entities; consequently, attention for the one cannot be conceived without attention for the other, while it is the same matrix of power that effects both a neutralisation of solicitude for others and the suppression of concern for nature.

In the 1940s, Adorno, together with Horkheimer, developed a theme that forms the guiding thread of *Dialectic of*

Enlightenment, namely that the *telos* of reason is the domination of nature. In this work, Adorno and Horkheimer describe the process of civilisation as having accompanied reason's narrowing to its instrumental form. This narrowing is simultaneously the condition of an endless extension during which reason asserts itself by enslaving its other, nature, and by assigning to each fact, to each being, a place in an overall plan which is one of calculation, efficiency and commodification. One of the book's fragments, titled 'Man and Beast', opens with the relatively conventional statement that 'throughout European history the idea of the human being has been expressed in contradistinction to the animal'.[52] But this is only to add that, 'today', in 1944, the difference with animals is posited once and for all, starkly. Domination has reached such completeness that the perpetual repetition of the splitting into two of man and animal (the animal in man) is no longer necessary. Internal nature is so well suppressed that no one can any longer find in it any air of familiarity with an external nature, which is itself completely tamed. This is why man is no longer able to experience 'the secret fear that it is itself enslaved to impotence, to death, to nature'.[53] As for nature – something still betrayed by certain bodies, those of Jews and of women – it has become unbearable and calls for brutality and destruction. Perceived as weakness and fragility, the drive that nature arouses is a sadistic one. Plus, the rational beings that we have all become see no reason at all to have any concern for beasts devoid of reason.

It should be noted that the aforementioned critique of Kant's neutralising of emotions in his conception of morality as freedom is, in Adorno's case, articulated in the idea that Kantian ethics represents the realisation of the bourgeois principle of domination of nature, particularly in that it requires the controlling of instinctual energies, that is, a mutilation of internal nature.[54]

But it is at an even deeper level, according to Adorno, that the rationality of the transcendental Kantian subject participates in deploying a logic of domination: 'The permanent *reductio ad hominem* of all appearance prepares cognition for purposes of internal and external dominance. Its supreme expression is the principle of unity, a principle borrowed from production, which has been split into partial acts.'[55] Reason extends by producing knowledge in the mode of technology, which 'aims to produce neither concepts nor images, nor the joy of understanding, but method, exploitation of the labour of others, capital'.[56] Indeed, the Kantian theory of reason, which, at bottom, is only interested in 'the field of application of scientific proposals', collaborates in this general exploitation of internal and external nature.

In care theories, the moral stance is defined as caring for a world that is both natural and cultural because it is the world in which we live. In the famous definition of care that she developed with Berenice Fisher, Joan Tronto thus posits a continuum between caring for others and caring for non-humans:

Caring is a *species activity that includes everything that we do to maintain, continue, and repair our 'world' so that we can live in it as well as possible.* That world includes our bodies, our selves, and our environment, all of which we seek to interweave in a complex, life-sustaining web.[57]

In the brief history of ethical theories of care, the path to a concern that, as sketched in the foregoing quote, is owed to external nature has been explored in several ways. Defining care as what maintains the thread of daily life in all circumstances, Sandra Laugier's meditation on care is articulated with a Wittgensteinian- and Cavellian-inspired reflection on the concept of form of life, with the aim of conceiving a sort of environmental care. From this perspective care is conceived as the care given to life as flow and as form; it aims to preserve a form of life of inseparable social and biological dimensions. The context of disasters, 'always both social and natural (there are bodies suffering, elements unleashed, but also the hand of man and the history of his culpable negligence)',[58] gives us particular insight into how care activities reweave the everyday, demonstrating a concern for sustaining lives, both human and non-human, which, multiply entangled, take their form from this interweaving.

An ethic of care also explores a conception of vulnerability as inherent in all beings with which we live, which is not the same as extending the model of human vulnerability to all living beings, but instead implies recognition of animal or even vegetable forms of life in their particularity. This conception targets a vulnerability from which our moral obligations derive; animal vulnerability, like human vulnerability, does not leave us 'the choice to respond, or like Bartleby, to prefer not to',[59] to quote Patricia Paperman. The thesis that a relationship is not some trait that, external to the human being's constitution, is added from the outside to that which comprises a human being, a thesis by which our care obligations can be grounded in our relational nature, is not necessarily limited to inter-human relationships; environmental care is born in, but also and especially arises from, relationships between dependent human beings and vulnerable external nature.[60]

Finally, several authors, in particular Val Plumwood, have denounced the systematic introduction into traditional ethics of an ontological discontinuity or separation between nature and human beings, which is supported and reinforced by a series of associated dualisms, the aforementioned dichotomies masculine/feminine, active/passive, objective/subjective, dichotomies which serve the moral disqualification of emotions.[61] For such traditional ethical theories, the definition of the human being is not to be sought on the side of what is shared with the natural and the animal (for example, the body, sexuality, reproduction, emotions, senses . . .), but on the side of what supposedly separates the human being from it, namely reason. For theorists of care, by contrast, neglecting the animal pole of the dichotomy thus established is tantamount to fostering a construction wherein animals, human bodies, and those who care for them, women, are victims. From this perspective, caring for some is at the same time a political gesture towards having respect for others.

Gaps

This exercise of comparison between two differing conceptions of moral dispositions must not, however, obscure significant differences in the social and political theories in which they are respectively embedded.

A major difference between these two conceptions concerns the normativity of the everyday; while both share an orientation towards the insignificant, Adorno's micrology is not the ordinary life of an ethic of care.

In care theories, ordinary everyday reality concerns an invisible but constant caring for others, which is broken only in extreme situations. Caring activities incessantly provide for and mend forms of life; without these activities such forms of life would be simply unsustainable. Therefore, 'what is commonplace is the fact that people care for others, care about them and thus ensure the everyday functioning of the world'.[62] The task of care theories, then, is precisely to bring to attention those ongoing practices which, because they are carried out by women and/or minority groups, are not visible, do not count for a great deal.

Far from being woven from gestures of attention, the ordinary life described by Adorno takes place in a world that is false or 'wrong' (*falsch*) through and through, in which it is

not possible to live a just life. As he puts it, 'Es gibt kein rich-
tiges Leben im falschen' (There is no right life in the wrong
world), and all of us are from the first entangled in a 'nexus
of complicity' (*Schuldzusammenhang*).[63] Unable to change this
world or extricate ourselves from it, we cannot do otherwise
than participate in the evil it represents. We are thus complicit
in, and guilty of, propping up this world. But 'the smooth
facade of everyday life' conceals this reality; for Adorno it is
the ordinary, that which is repeated, which, by creating familiarity with the world as it is, erases the scandal this world
constitutes. Adorno justifies his use of exaggeration in writing
and reasoning by the need to break the force of normality that
everyday life generates: 'I have exaggerated the sombre side,
following the maxim that only exaggeration *per se* today can
be the medium of truth.'[64]

In other words, while both theoretical corpuses can be
seen to engage in an exercise of unveiling, the worlds thereby
revealed are profoundly antithetical: for care theories, this
world is one whose texture is moral, is made up of an infinity
of small moral gestures, while for Adorno it is one in which
the very possibility of the moral gesture is non-existent, or
survives only in islets, and which offers nothing but a chance
to live 'less wrongly'.[65]

Correlatively, as caring coincides with the perpetual mend-
ing of the ordinary world, care theories do not take up the
task of conceiving this world's destruction, nor even its radical
transformation. In Adorno, by contrast, the reproduction of
society, the propping up of our way of life as it is, is simply a
consequence of the condition of powerlessness that characterises the contemporary individual.

One theme that runs through Adorno's writing specifically
highlights the disparity with theories of care: a clear indis-
position towards pity. In the excursus devoted to 'Juliet or

Enlightenment and Morality' from *Dialectic of Enlightenment*, the book's authors juxtapose two antithetical assertions. First, they write, 'Sade and Nietzsche realized that once Reason had been formalized pity was left behind as a kind of sensuous awareness of the identity of general and particular, as a naturalized mediation.'[66] And second, that 'By limiting the abolition of injustice to fortuitous love of one's neighbour, pity accepts as unalterable the law of universal estrangement which it would like to alleviate.'[67] By proscribing pity normatively, the individual may well be freed from the burden of her moral intuitions, but relying on pity implies that one surrender the moral act to contingency and give up on making one's issue part of a wider moral and political practice. This theme is one to which Adorno would return some twenty years later in *Problems of Moral Philosophy*, where he refutes an ethics of compassion on the grounds that it merely softens distress while leaving intact the conditions of its production: 'the pity you express for someone always contains an element of injustice towards that person; he experiences not just our pity but also the impotence and specious character of the compassionate act.'[68]

'Pity' is a word that theorists of care generally avoid using as such, doubtless owing to its heavy Christian connotation, but also in order to avert the ambivalence that the philosophical tradition lends the notion, as both desire for power and expectation of gratitude. The fact remains that pity is a particular form of concern for others and that ethical theories of care leave its politically dark side unexplored.

Adorno's critique of this moral feeling – a critique of its arbitrary and conservative nature – sheds light on and emends the naivety that accompanied the birth, in the 1980s, of care theories, which were conceived as a feminist response to the ultraliberalism under way in Anglo-Saxon countries, yet did not investigate the way in which they actually permitted this ultraliberalism. Indeed, despite the emphasis placed on work in their thinking, the majority of theorists of care, who almost never refer to Marxist feminism from the 1970s, leave unthought the way care work is embedded in the capitalist order.[69] There is no appropriation or refining of the reflection on 'reproductive work', of the labour of looking after human needs. Within Marxist feminism, this embedding led some to denounce a reductionist definition of work as limited to the sphere of production, since under the conditions of capitalism only work that creates exchange value appears as such[70]; specifically, Marxist feminism made it clear that, by allowing for the reproduction of labour power, reproductive work underlies the creation of exchange value.

Naturally, care work is deemed to be socially necessary work (as Tronto and Fischer's foregoing definition makes explicit: 'caring is a species activity'), but this work is not considered in its organisation by and for a particular political economy. Its exteriority, long total, now only partial, vis-à-vis the market, is thus not analysed as a condition of possibility for this same market (but simply for its consequences in terms of distributive and statutory justice for women). Care work is not theorised as a condition for the existence of wage labour, the accumulation of surplus value and the functioning of capitalism as such. Theories of care work and Adorno's philosophy thus also differ in the extent to which they challenge the capitalist form of life and analyse its underlying ruses and paradoxes.

Lastly, an important divergence emerges thanks to the centrality that Adorno attributes to self-criticism in his moral philosophy. It is not that theorists of care simply relegate the theme of self-reflection to the shadows, since the moral voice they describe is coextensive with a moral *questioning* (and not with the enunciation or application of a rule), and since they evoke the notion that the risk of acting poorly necessarily provokes anxiety. Nevertheless, in Adorno's moral philosophy critical self-reflection constitutes a unique and recurrent problem, because, as he says, 'true injustice is always to be found at the precise point where you put yourself in the right and other people in the wrong'.[71] Adorno questions the very idea of a pure intention to act morally, arguing, as his critique of the ethics of conviction has taught us, that what appears to be thus and so is often the result of repressed drives or feelings of guilt. But the self-criticism to which he remains committed also implies guarding against the tendency to 'hold fast to what we think we have learnt from experience',[72] a tendency that, by contrast, theories of care call to embrace. Self-criticism involves confronting the modalities of one's own participation in a wrong world, developing a form of 'modesty' (*Bescheidenheit*), which is the only virtue that regularly recurs in his writings, and is understood as a resistance to the feeling of one's own infallibility. This theme is not brought up as a simple corrective measure. The moral injunction to examine oneself critically is so strong that, in the concluding lecture of *Problems of Moral Philosophy*, Adorno ends up positing that 'the element of self-reflection has today become the true heir to what used to be called moral categories'.[73]

We must now turn to Adorno's reflection on the capitalist form of life, the threads of which I unravel in order to flesh out more fully his conception of concern for others and the type of socio-political neutralisation to which it is subjected.

2 The Empire of Coldness

Adorno's arguments about 'bourgeois coldness' suggest that we conceive of the moral agent as one whose vulnerability is socially produced, which is to say inherent in the fact that one is likely to be caught in a relationship with oneself and the world that prevents one from perceiving others' moral expectations and suffering. Bourgeois coldness is reflected in an indifference towards others inherent in the pursuit of one's own interests, an inability to identify with others, a hasty subscription to the inevitable and a carefully maintained narrowing of existence to the private—the 'general subjective mechanisms without which Auschwitz would have hardly been possible'.[1] It is not only passivity in the face of others' suffering or expectations; it is combined with a 'willingness to connive with power',[2] and to bow down to force as if it were a norm.

To define the vulnerability of which bourgeois coldness is the result, Adorno evokes phenomena throughout his work, though without necessarily articulating them with one another, that are inherent in capitalism and that commit us, or constrain us, to 'forget' others. This highly multiform thesis of forgetting, which partly blends with his theory of reification, requires careful examination because it offers a key to understanding the origin and nature that he attributes to moral dispositions.

Withering of Experience, Commensurability, Fetishism and Self-Preservation. Forgetting Others

Adorno brings to light a multitude of behavioural patterns, social dynamics and institutionalised forms that limit our ways of perceiving things and people, and converge to ensure that the only possible attitude in the 'administered' world we live in is indifference.

Withering of Lived Experience

Following Walter Benjamin, Adorno describes a withering of lived experience,[3] which he sees as one of the main forces in the absence of concern for others. According to Benjamin, that which is lived can be transformed into experience only if a significant relationship can be established between the past and the future, the personal and the collective. Full experience, *Erfahrung*, is inseparable from an anchoring of lived experience in history, such as we have experienced it, thanks to stable narrative models, and in the light of older horizons of experience. By contrast, the media-driven reconstruction of the event as information works to produce a content made available to everyone in an instrumental way. The event thus becomes rigorously fixed and sterilised; it has no other consistency than that of the present and leaves no traces. It causes a brief state of shock only; information merely shakes up consciousness. Thus carrying no meaning, the event cannot be sedimented into experience. Similarly, the organisation of work in a factory, which alters each of the senses, isolates the worker from all experience, replacing memory by conditioned response, know-how by repetition. Practice no longer has any meaning. *Erfahrungen* then give way to atomised *Erlebnisse*, raw lived experiences,[4] which are more a matter of convulsion and trauma than of intelligible moments of existence; they become accidents from which we must defend ourselves. In these conditions, people aspire 'to free themselves from experience'.[5] Thanks to this withering a profound change is brought about in the relationship to the other, time and nature.

Similarly for Adorno (and Horkheimer), the individual is reduced to 'a mere succession of instantaneous presents, which leave no trace'.[6] Having no market value *Erfahrung* is henceforth proscribed, while the past is without meaning for the present, or is enjoined not to have any. Presented in one of the concluding notes and sketches to *Dialectic of Enlightenment*, one devoted to our relationship with our dead, this diagnosis leads to the observation that mourning, now a mere social formality, can no longer be experienced. No longer able to be lived, loss gives way to the disengaged carrying out of rites.

The causal force that Benjamin attributes to the media with regard to the generalisation of *Erlebnisse* is attributed by Adorno to the culture industry, especially when it comes to music. Multiplying the basic musical enticements, the music industry conditions the ear, in such a way that reflexive reaction replaces reflected experience in listening to music. The relationship to music thus becomes atomised, characterised by discontinuity and an inability to perform syntheses. A mode of hearing is developed that ignores the fact that there is nothing isolated in music, that 'everything [in music] becomes what it is in memory and in expectation through its physical contiguity with its neighbour and its mental connection with what is distant from it'.[7] Adorno thus describes a withering of musical experience, which, in echo of Benjamin's description of experience in general as having been wrenched from time, no longer organised by processes of recollection and expectation.

The culture industry, with its increasingly strong connections with propaganda and advertising, also transforms language; the repetition of syntagma and slogans in films and radio shows supports their rapid assimilation, such that 'language takes on the coldness which hitherto was peculiar to billboards and the advertising sections of newspapers'.[8] As a result, the part of experience that used to bind words to people disappears. Repeated without being understood, used for the automatic effects they have come to produce, words are no longer the site of a 'sedimentary experience'.

Beyond its neutralisation through the culture industry, *Erfahrung* also becomes paralysed due to the shock of individual life against a deadening technology of power. The two world wars, with their completely mechanical, motorised texture, brought about such incongruity 'between the body and mechanical warfare' that real experience was made impossible.[9] The recollection of what, in the series of violent events, has been lived through is hampered, or, more accurately, struck with impotence.

As aforementioned, Adorno's work engages in a critique of the false immediacy of singular experience, on which it is pernicious[10] to rely, since the capitalist form of life gives it as unshaped, as the throwing and jolting of an unaffected subjectivity, which is actually always-already subject to an intrusion of socially ordered modes of behaviour and apprehension. Precisely 'where the subject feels altogether sure of itself – in primary experience – it will be least subjective'.[11] Nevertheless, even if experience as such does not offer access to any emancipation or proof of autonomy, such poverty of experience can have only negative moral effects, which we learn from observing individuals such as torturers, or even persons who are simply manipulative: they are actually incapable of 'true experience'.[12] Within this withering of experience, encounters with others are bereft of meaning, devoid of consequence; they are just clashes that do no more than 'happen'. By structurally breaking the linearity and sequencing of perception, the possibilities for integrating moments, expectations and important events fritter away. If it is true that experience offers no guarantee of right knowledge, no reliable resource for orienting oneself in relationships with others, its mutation into *Erlebnis* thingifies all interactions with others and their properties, and what is simply unknown becomes foreign.

More, the link between indifference to others and the generalisation of raw experience also stems from the fact that late capitalism's atrophying of experience, far from individualising the subject in the face of others, far from giving her uniqueness, renders the subject interchangeable and standardised.

Commensurability and Interchangeability

The administered world has eliminated the possibility of behaving, or even being seen, as a singular being. This is because the model established by exchange within capitalism has generalised to such an extent that any object, but also any subject, can be exchanged for another. The object is, in its qualities and realisations, comparable, able to be measured against any other. As stated in *Dialectic of Enlightenment* 'bourgeois society is ruled by equivalence. It makes dissimilar things comparable by reducing them to abstract quantities'.[13] In exchange, non-identical individuals become commensurable with each other, which is to say identical.

In so doing, capitalism simply unfolds a logic that is intrinsic to reason and its tireless work of dominating nature; the levelling abstraction it establishes, according to which everything in nature is reproducible, comes to be coupled with the development of an industry that materialises and organises this reproducibility. Capitalism is also based on a modern quantifying science, to which sociology belongs, and which, for example, by producing typologies, brings the individual back to a simple datum, compilable with others, generalisable.

Empirical research on social issues takes at face value, and helps to support the idea of, social atoms 'capable of quantitative variation, but certainly not disparity'.[14]

More generally still, interchangeability and commensurability, which the exchange relation establishes, are counterparts to identifying thought, which, proceeding via the concept, brings the non-identical to heel. And as thought operates through concepts, the first pages of *Negative Dialectics* give us to understand that 'to think means to identify'; the concept slips in front of the thing and substitutes itself for the thing, since, unable to grasp the non-conceptual and the particular, it eliminates them. A concept tells us what a given thing participates in, what it is a copy of, thus erasing what constitutes the singularity of this something. While identifying thought exists independently of market logic, it spreads only to the extent that the relation of exchange enforces its implementation in all spheres of activity. It is objectively and compulsively realised equivalence that is the perpetual matrix of a form of thought hostile to singularity. Not only does the process of abstraction realised by philosophy take place in the real society of exchanges, but more profoundly, 'The principle of exchange, the reduction of human labour to an abstract general concept of average labour-time, is primordially related to the principle of identification. Exchange is the social model of the principle, and without the principle there would be no exchange; it is through exchange that non-identical individuals and performances become commensurable and identical.'[15] The principle of identity has thus attained its current position of universal domination only in so far as bourgeois society is shaped by exchange.

This is of course reflected first of all in the fact that science and the state reduce the human being to a statistical element that fellow humans assess according to market value. Yet it is the whole form of capitalist life as such that is imbued with, and accomplishes, this generalised commensurability.

Accordingly, the idea of equality itself derives from bourgeois society's principle of the organisation of exchange; the equality that prevails or even is simply hoped for is that of partners in an exchange – signatories of a contract. Yet, Adorno tells us, the 'introduction of contracts into questions of intellectual solidarity' nevertheless 'remains an instrument for the suspension of equality and for subjugation, and *presupposes a condition in which individual subjects are in mortal enmity with one another*, by means of which competitive society becomes increasingly like the primal horde'.[16] Generalised interchangeability infuses political values and grammars, putting them at the service of bourgeois coldness; far from being a principle of justice, equality is only a principle of indifference.

Adorno's view of psychoanalysis is a highly ambivalent one, in that he sees it, too, as a device by which the immeasurable, that which is considered abnormal or chaotic, in particular conflicts between the drives, becomes commensurable: suffering is transformed into a symptom.[17] The abysses of the ego becomes levelled and compartmentalised into mass-market products, my disturbances come to guarantee my conformity and provide the tool of my comparability.

It can even be said that the capitalist form of life coincides with generalising of a 'commodity form' that accompanies the institutionalisation of exchange. In keeping with the furrow ploughed by Karl Marx, this is the proposition put forward by Alfred Sohn-Rethel, in texts that were collected and published only in 1978 under the title *Warenform und Denkform*, several manuscripts to which Adorno had been privy as of 1937. According to Sohn-Rethel, the origin of the *forms* – and not only the contents – of consciousness, the origin of grids for the prehension of data that provide a sensory perception, is historical and lies in the generalisation of exchange. Adorno seems to fully embrace this idea when he emphasises, in an exchange with Horkheimer while conducting preparatory work for *Dialectic of Enlightenment*, that it should be proved in the forthcoming book that 'any concept of knowledge that starts from the subject is always an exchange of equivalents [. . .] The idea of just exchange is already found in the concept of adequacy.'[18]

More fundamentally, rather than Georg Lukács, it is perhaps to Sohn-Rethel that Adorno owes the primacy of the category of exchange for characterising the capitalist form of life, in contrast with other Marxist categories, such as exploitation, abstract work or social classes. In Sohn-Rethel he finds an explanation of abstraction in terms of exchange rather than of work, where in Marx the driving force behind abstraction is work.[19] If Adorno sometimes agrees that the origin of the principle of exchange lies in the abstraction of work, as when he characterises it as 'the reduction of human labor to an abstract general concept of average labour time',[20] or when he evokes the metamorphosis of labour power into a commodity that permeates human beings through and through by objectifying their impulses so as to make them commensurable,[21] it is not abstract work but exchange that returns on page after page of his work. In his preface to Sohn-Rethel, Anselm Jappe puts it as follows: 'exchange becomes a reality apart, separate in relation to labour and use. It is purely social.'[22]

Exchange even works to ensure the social link itself: the circulation of goods constitutes the link between all things (*nexus rerum*), renewing abstraction at the level of each interaction. It is therefore society as a whole that can be qualified as abstract.[23] For Sohn-Rethel, Lukács and Adorno alike, the abstraction of exchange constitutes society both 'conceptually and in reality'.[24]

Finally, for both Sohn-Rethel and Adorno, exchange produces forms of thought that allow a conception of nature as an objectal world opposed to the human world. 'All the concepts resulting from abstraction-exchange have in common the timeless and anhistorical character that also defines this concept of nature as a world of quantifying objects. In abstraction-exchange, society erases itself.'[25]

The generalisation of the exchange form hinders solidarity, erases singularity, fits human beings for the market and as always-already instrumentalised for it, and posits nature as distinct from and opposed to the human – it is thus undoubtedly sufficient in itself to render impossible any form of attention to others; the Nazi camps, which Adorno sees as the natural children of capitalism and of the type of reason it embodies, are the extreme proof of this, in so far as it was not 'the individual [*Individuum*] [who] died in the concentration camps, but rather the specimen'.[26] At Auschwitz a complete liquidation of the individual was carried out, with effects on moral life that are plain to see. Commensurability presumes that relations between individuals degrade into relations between things; as Adorno puts it with Horkheimer in *Dialectic of Enlightenment*, within the fully accomplished capitalist form of life, 'Being is apprehended in terms of manipulation and administration. Everything – including the individual human being, not to mention the animal – becomes a repeatable, replaceable process, a mere example of the conceptual models of the system.'[27] Thus, even responding with benevolence in the same way to everyone as absolutely interchangeable, even the indiscriminate showing of kindness, can only be a manifestation of its opposite – coldness.[28]

In its attempt to uncover the social causes of bourgeois coldness, Adorno's reflection thus focuses on a generalised and constraining *form*, rather than on a mystifying *discourse* or set of false representations that would commit human beings to adopt attitudes apt to serve the reproduction of the capitalist order. Says Adorno, 'If the standard structure of society is the exchange form, its rationality constitutes people: what they are for themselves, what they think they are, is secondary.'[29] The very idea of internalisation, whether of norms or models, is out of place, because 'this mechanism does not even permit the constitution of a stable subjectivity';[30] by constraining one to reciprocal instrumentalisation, the exchange form replaces such subjectivity. Above all, to criticise ideology as practised by Enlightenment philosophers and their heirs, who make naive postulations about the 'machinations woven by the powerful',[31] is problematic – it presumes a posture based on the belief that it is enough 'to bring order into consciousness, for order to be brought into society'.[32] The category of ideology bears relevance only if, instead of referring to a reality radically distinct from the commodity form, it constitutes a sedimentation of this form, making it heavier, more palpable. Adorno thus notes that what identifying thought does is to suggest an adequation between the thing and its concept, thus blinding us to reality. On this basis, he posits that 'identity is the primal form of ideology'.[33] What matters is that both thing and concept are characterised by their objectivity.

At times we thus see appear the idea that the exchange-form is duplicated by an ideological veil, which takes on the sense of a doubling of being (*étant*) that works as a celebration of the latter. More specifically, this falsification is envisaged as a product of the culture industry, in which coldness is praised as being proper to a salutary and vigorous life: 'Far from merely concealing the suffering under the cloak of improvised comradeship, the culture industry stakes its company pride on looking it manfully in the eye and acknowledging it with unflinching composure. This posture of steadfast endurance justifies the world which that posture makes necessary. Such is the world – so hard, yet therefore so wonderful, so healthy.'[34]

Phantasmagoria and Fetishism

In the same spirit, Adorno couches an explanation of coldness in the categories of phantasmagoria and fetishism, describing thus both the reduction of imagination and the trap that imagination represents by permitting the fake enchantment of the world. According to this thesis, the force of enchantment of the outward form of the commodity, the ensuing attribution of a quasi-mythical origin and power to certain things or phenomena that are nevertheless perfectly social, perpetuates mutual disinterest and generalised moral aridity. For these phantasmagoria conceal not only the traces of human labour that have permitted the commodity to come to existence, and with it the accumulation of capital, but also what bodies suffer by way of coercion and violence. It thus erases all traces of 'the human' and of its due. But it is further able to create the illusion that, within this completely petrified reality, the human is keenly present, making any concern about this reality unnecessary. This is the function of the immense phantasmagoria that Adorno believes Wagner's music is. Inundating the senses, unifying them by duplicating the same content, it proceeds by intoxication, thereby reheating the reified and alienated relationships of human beings and lending them the appearance of being ever human relationships.[35]

If these very Benjaminian themes of phantasmagoria and fetishism are rather present in Adorno's pre-war writings,[36] much later we also find, for example in 'Educating after

Auschwitz', written in 1966, a denunciation of technology fetishism on the grounds that coldness can be its only correlate. In Adorno's view those who tend to consider technology – that is, the set of means aimed at conserving the human species – as an end and a force in itself, who tend to be bewitched by it and to forget that it ought to serve human ends, can only be 'perfectly cold beings, forced to radically deny the possibility of love, and to withdraw their love from other individuals before it even flourishes'.[37]

However, here again, there is no strong dissimilarity between these phenomena of enchantment and the idea of an objective and generalised 'form'. This is the whole meaning of the criticism that Adorno addresses to Benjamin for the content that he gives the notion of phantasmagoria by tacking it onto 'behaviours' or contents of consciousness: for Adorno, only 'if phantasmagoria are treated as an objectively historical-philosophical category rather than as a "vision" on the part of social characters'[38] can they reveal something of the administered world. Similarly, in 'The Fetish-Character in Music' (1938) he distinguishes between the effects of musical fetishism, psychological satisfactions, and the origin of this fetishism, which is not psychological. Exchange value is consumed, causing affects, but this happens even before the consumer's consciousness has grasped the specific qualities of the musical good being listened to – this follows from its character as a commodity.[39]

In short, according to Adorno, both things and the concrete and material organisation of the world participate in holding together social practices and institutions, the relationship to the world and ways of perceiving, and the attitudes and behavioural dispositions that constitute our lives. Bourgeois coldness is therefore not a psychological phenomenon; it is as much social as objective. It nevertheless (or in this way) infuses bourgeois subjectivity.

Self-Preservation

Adorno repeatedly associates coldness with another logic: it is inseparable from self-preservation. Regardless of the mystifications that instil indifference, the withering of experience and the false objectivity that results from generalised commensurability, coldness is, at an ontological level, required as a resource of self-preservation, whose primacy is progressively imposed in keeping with the history of the deployment of reason and domination of nature. Coldness becomes the only possible mode of action: 'Whoever imagines that as a product of this society he is free of the bourgeois coldness harbors illusions about himself as much as about the world; without such coldness one could not live.'[40]

The imperative of self-preservation establishes reason as a blend of having a sense of reality, precisely assessing power relations, and a capacity for adaptation that guards against paying any attention to others or having any concern for an existence other than one's own.

Coldness thus undergoes a process of phylogenesis, which we are told about in *Dialectic of Enlightenment*. This book's first chapters present the mythical powers as a necessary stage for learning an individuality that hardens to the extent that it resists these powers and develops itself in an effort of self-preservation. Adorno and Horkheimer make Odysseus, who suffers friction with a brutal world that obliges brutality, first of all towards himself, the first representation of the human's becoming-subject: 'The mechanism of adaptation to hardening realities simultaneously engenders a hardening within the individual: the more realistic he becomes, the more he feels reduced to a thing, the more deadened he becomes, and the more senseless his whole "realism".'[41] But to constitute oneself as a pure instrumental intelligence dominating nature also implies the development of a trenchant egocentrism.

The story of Odysseus, as a figure of the myth in which reason already arises (and with it the motif of exchange, which invests the sacrifice, which has the effect of dethroning the gods), is then a story of the forgetting of others: 'The universal socialisation for which the globetrotter Odysseus [. . .]. was attended from the first by the absolute loneliness which at the end of the bourgeois era is becoming overt. Radical socialization means radical alienation.'[42] Odysseus is faced with the constitutive choice of bourgeois society: cheat or go under, a choice that makes others appear to him as either simply 'enemies' or 'allies'.[43]

The next chapter, dedicated to Sade's Juliette, describes the Enlightenment's contempt for pity, remorse, commiseration, tenderness and, more broadly, for everything that does not resemble a morality of mastery and domination. It therefore relates a step in the process of reducing reason to its instrumental dimension, after that of Odysseus. If the latter prefigured the calculating bourgeois, Clairwill and Juliette announce fascism, in which coldness is not simply present, there, but is made into a mark of greatness.

Thus has human history to date been one with the history of the advent of coldness.

In this history, philosophy has certainly played its part. Adorno's multifaceted critique of Kantianism and its conception of will as a pure affirmation of reason aims notably at an abstraction that expounds on a disastrous culture of indifference. The part devoted to Sade in the *Dialectic of Enlightenment* therefore also teaches us how the increasing formalisation of theoretical reason contaminates practical reason. This process, contrary to what Kant had in mind, has no more affinity with morality than with immorality.

More broadly still, modern moral philosophy, Adorno claims, has turned mutual indifference into the very condition of morality and justice; the idea of a moral norm is built on the presupposition of a lack of interest in others (which appears in reasoning only as a pure abstraction from the other individual), and arranged as a correction made to my personal interest. Therefore, as Jay Bernstein points out, all the moral and political laws thought out and established within this framework 'secretly transmit coldness as a morally legitimate stance toward others'.[44] If bourgeois morality demands consideration of others, this consideration requires an emotional withdrawal, a disengagement, in the very act of taking them into account.

The indifference carried by the centuries-old movement of perfection of the logic of self-preservation nevertheless takes on a socio-historical specificity in bourgeois subjectivity and the form of life of late capitalism, thanks to the generalisation of the form of exchange and a developing culture industry that presents brutality as an unproblematic experience.

From this point of view, if the advent of bourgeois coldness is made possible by forms of thought and practices that have sedimented throughout the history of the West, and more particularly in the later phases of capitalism, the disappearance of certain bourgeois mores and rules, having suffered a serious battering by Nazism, paradoxically constitutes the completion of the generalisation of this coldness. We thus find it underscored in *Minima Moralia* that

Behind the pseudo-democratic dismantling of ceremony, of old-fashioned courtesy, of the useless conversation suspected, not even unjustly, of being idle gossip, behind the seeming clarification and transparency of human relations that no longer admit anything undefined, naked brutality is ushered in.[45]

The social conventions of politeness appear in retrospect as having been able to avoid contracting individuality around sheer self-preservation. The absence of any dressing up of relations between people, their simplification for the sole purpose of their effectiveness, makes it possible to treat people as things, leaving nothing over. Beyond the regulated conduct of the bourgeoisie, Kantian respect itself, which, in so far as its presumed impartiality entails a real lack of affection, an embodied disinterest in the concrete other, nevertheless served as a kind of corset: it was the site of a form of control of the bourgeoisie of its own class. Fascism, on the other hand, 'which by its iron discipline relieves its peoples of the burden of moral feelings, no longer needs to observe any discipline'.[46]

Coldness attains its perfect realisation as soon as it leaves behind its bourgeois finery, which nevertheless contributed to entrenching this coldness in subjectivities and the capitalist form of life.

What results from this set of arrangements is that individuals are for each other *at best* means, recruited as part of a strategic calculation towards a given end. The exchange-form, the generalisation of raw experiences, the phantasmagoria of capital and the subordination of moral consciousness to the imperative of self-preservation, all determine an individual's evaluations and allocation of respect and attention. Society then comes to be composed of dissociated monads who 'balk at their real dependence as a species as well as at the collective aspect of all forms and contents of their consciousness'.[47] What late capitalism undermines, then, is unconditional attention to others as much as the willingness to perceive their expectations and needs.

For Adorno and Horkheimer, this perversion of the relationship with oneself and others specifically takes the form of a neutralisation of the ability to be affected by the suffering of others, and a blindness to the pain and sorrow caused by the mastery of nature, a blindness which they see as one of the conditions for progress: 'But the perennial dominion over nature, medical and nonmedical technology, derives its strength from such blindness; it would be made possible only by forgetting.'[48] And, they add: 'All reification is *forgetting*.'[49]

What Adorno therefore singles out under the name of reification (although other meanings are also attributed to the word) are processes that prevent, in an undifferentiated way among members of the administered society, the development or maintenance of a certain relationship to the world and the moral dispositions that go with it.

Reflections on the Thesis of 'Forgetting'

Adorno's diagnosis mobilises not only the word 'forgetting' but also the vocabulary of suffocation, the atrophying of moral competences or feelings, the mutilation, evisceration, dismemberment of moral subjectivity, and indeed the castration of perception. It would thus seem to postulate the idea that concern for others underlies the normal functioning of intersubjectivity, broken by the authoritarian exercise of power and the investing by capitalist social relations in interindividual relations. Other formulations, such as the idea, which appears in *Minima Moralia*, that human beings are sometimes forced to deceive themselves, to develop argumentative strategies to neutralise the empathy that may arise when they have to kill – 'it's only an animal' – may seem to indicate a concern for others, certainly repressible, but always-already there.[50] This opens the path to a possible misinterpretation of Adorno's thought.

The Category of Forgetting: More Political Than Cognitive

According to Axel Honneth's reading of Adorno's work, the human being's concern for others is originary; it constitutes the condition of possibility of establishing a relationship with the world, whereas its fragility lies essentially in the possibility of its unlearning. In *Reification*, Honneth defines recognition of others as a primordial form of relationship to the world, drawing on the concepts of practical engagement in John Dewey, the engaged relationship in Lukács and acknowledgement in Cavell. Above all, availing himself of certain aphorisms from *Minima Moralia*, he finds in Adorno the idea that it is only through imitation, permitted by a form of attachment, love and even libidinal investment, that we develop an ability to reason, in that we gradually learn to relate ourselves to the perspective of others on the world by imitating these others. This process is then likely to be forgotten, which results in an essentially cognitive distortion of the relationship with others. If we follow such a reading, reification then comes to signify 'a "recentering" of man, who, according to the standard of exchange, unlearns how to perceive the world from the perspective of those intentions and wishes whose significance had originally emerged through imitation'.[51]

Along this line (the epigraph to *Reification* is 'all reification is (a) forgetting'), Honneth develops the idea of an originary non-cognitive stance towards things and persons, defined by the fact that we experience situations in such a way that we take *care* to maintain a relationship with our environment:

our actions do not primarily have the character of an affectively neutral, cognitive stance toward the world, but rather that of an affirmative, existentially coloured style of caring comportment. In living, we constantly concede to the situational circumstances of our world a value of their own, which brings us to be concerned with our relationship to them.[52]

Reification occurs when this engagement in the world disappears or is forgotten; therewith, we lose 'the ability to understand immediately the behavioural expressions of other persons as making claims on us – as demanding that we react in an appropriate way'.[53] We are ever able to perceive the expressions of others, but no longer that which binds us to them; yet it is this feeling that is necessary for us to truly understand the demands and expectations of others.

In Honneth's appropriation of Adorno, the fragility of concern for others thus proceeds first of all from its exposure to institutionalised models for apprehending others that are radically instrumental, models which, by their prevalence and ubiquity, neutralise an originary competence.

Honneth's theory of reification is notoriously problematic for several reasons, both in itself and to the extent that it claims to be following in Adorno's footsteps. First, Honneth completely decouples the reification of the mechanisms and the effects of capitalism. He thus explicitly reproaches Lukács for the specious positing of an equivalence exchanges of goods and reification, a weakness that the conception of reification as forgetting (of one's primary affective engagement with the world) is supposed to overcome. By turning reification into a primarily psychological phenomenon involving the suffocation and instrumentalisation of inner lived experiences, Honneth disconnects intersubjectivity from the social and objectal dimensions of interaction and dispenses with the examination of the forms of power that determine it.

Second, for Honneth reification comes about because knowledge cuts itself off from its dependence on recognition and is specifically subject to delusions about this 'independence'; it *'deludes itself that it has become autonomous of all non-epistemic prerequisites'*.[54] In other words, reification occurs when in our operations of knowledge the trace is lost of what they owe to an attitude of recognition, when the consciousness vanishes of all that results from a committed participation in the world. Obstructing access to originary experience, masking or denying it, reification, in Honneth, becomes a loss of the conditions of possibility of our actions, and even of our being.

If *Reification* thus contains a reflection on attention, its object is not attention to the other, its affects and distress. At issue is not a refinement or intensification of the empathic moment, but an attention to oneself and the conditions of one's own access to knowledge and moral deliberation. The question of this interpretation's fidelity to the Adornian legacy, then, arises in so far as reification here becomes a problem of the rectitude of knowledge and its conditions, a breach of some practical presupposition, a lack of the lucidity that is our due. The considerations that motivate Adorno's reflection on forgetting are unequivocally of a moral[55] and political nature. The core of the problem of 'forgetting' is not cognitive. Pace Honneth, who partly adopts Martin Seel's interpretation of Adorno,[56] Adorno does not denounce forgetting because the relevance of our conceptual thinking depends on our awareness of thought's original connection to the object of a drive.[57] The heart of the problem is rather that 'it is part of the mechanism of domination to forbid recognition of the suffering it produces'.[58]

The well-known association made between reification and forgetting in *Dialectic of Enlightenment* is not the first instance of it in Adorno. In a letter he addressed to Benjamin on 29 February 1940, he provides a striking formulation of this association on the basis of the aforementioned deterioration of *Erfahrung* into *Erlebnis*. He asks: 'Is it not the case that the real task here is to bring the entire opposition between sensory experience [*Erlebnis*] and experience proper [*Erfahrung*] into relation with a dialectical theory of forgetting?'[59] For *Erfahrung* implies an involuntary memory, which cannot arise without a moment of forgetting. This is what Benjamin himself had highlighted in his essay on Baudelaire, by articulating aura and experience with

Proustian involuntary memory. Involuntary memory allows us to experience objects that we did not really experience during our original encounter with them. It is then that we are struck by them in their singularity. Raw experience, which Adorno associates with reification, is also based on forgetting, but on another form of it. The forgetting that is a condition of possibility of *Erfahrung* is an 'epic' forgetting, while the forgetting that accompanies *Erlebnis* is a reflex forgetting, both immediate and continuous. Objects become merely thing-like the moment that various of their aspects are caught within this latter forgetting. Reification results from the fact that objects 'are fixed without the continued presence of all their other aspects'.[60] In *Prisms* (1955) this idea again emerges, when Adorno evokes the threat that a brutal and mechanical forgetting presents to *Erfahrung*, a danger that the poetry of modernity, that of George, Hofmannsthal, Baudelaire, sought to resist: 'The passionate effort to express oneself in language, keeping banality at a distance, is the attempt, however hopeless, to extricate experience from its mortal enemy, which engulfs it in late bourgeois society – forgetting.'[61] In other words, these poets have tried to stem the erosion of language, a vector of reification in that it withdraws the means by which we might recall particular aspects of things and human beings. The erosion of language then fixes them all in place unremittingly.

Adorno returned to the theme of reification as forgetting again in 1968, in one of his last lectures, published in *Introduction to Sociology*. Here once again, he links reification to time and to an experience no longer able to be had. The passage in question is one in which he accuses sociology of focusing exclusively on the moment, on the immediate. Quoting his own statement 'all reification is (a) forgetting', he further unfolds this train of thought as follows: 'and critique (with which sociology should merge) really means the same as remembrance – that is, mobilizing in phenomena that by

which they have become, and thereby recognizing the possibility that they might have become, and could therefore be,
something different'.[62] Sociology can only claim to be critical
if it requires the remembrance of all the non-actualised aspects
of a process or an event.

Perhaps there is, indeed, in Adorno, 'an internal context
between morality and knowledge',[63] as Honneth argues: it
is located not in the link between denial of recognition and
failures in our cognitive access to the objective world, but
instead in the effects of these on our relationship to *others* and
to things. As it is suggested in *Minima Moralia*, 'Is not memory
inseparable from love, which seeks to preserve what yet must
pass away?'[64]

What Adorno envisages against the grain, indeed that to
which reification prevents access, is what we owe in terms
of *attention*, of *concern* to all aspects of an object or person, to
everything that is or would have been possible, to everything
that has been and is no longer (or no longer in this form),
to the suffering that we inflict or that is simply there, to all
the facets that make a person a singular being. Forgetting
means not taking into account the continuous presence of all
these aspects; it means not figuring them among what is said
to count. The idea of reification thus makes it possible to
describe an economy of attention as inadequate as it is wrong,
falsch, in the twofold sense permitted by the German language, and with which Adorno already plays when he speaks
of 'wrong life'.[65]

Honneth's development of his own theory of reification
oscillates between the thesis of unlearning and the interpretation of forgetting as a loss, as a suspension of attention: 'To the
extent to which in our acts of cognition we lose sight of the
fact that these acts owe their existence to our having taken up
an antecedent recognitional stance.'[66] However, he seems to

attribute to Adorno the sole thesis of unlearning, which presupposes an original competence now lost. This can be seen, beyond his recurrent use of the term *verlernen*, in his efforts to extract from Adorno's writings a fascination with childhood, and the idea that overcoming reification would coincide with the return to the empathic relationship that the child is supposed to maintain with objects and persons through imitation. The liberating recollection is then a recollection of infancy, a revivification of the emotional and libidinal investment in the environment that characterises this age. According to Honneth, this idea of childhood provides Adorno with the basis for a critique of the capitalist form of life,[67] and engages a return to an untouched state prior to determination.

Understanding the Adornian thesis of reification as an argument about unlearning, then, seems inappropriate not only because of the fact that the problem Adorno seeks to circumscribe is more moral and political than cognitive: it is because it omits the fact that reification is not thought of as a deinstallation, or a methodically ordered disintegration of an original, natural or ontic human competence.

The Human Being, a Figure without Substrate

It should first be recalled that if we rely on Adorno for a conception of the human as a static being on whom alterations are imposed by external influences, and as adapting to external conditions of production and of life, to the existence of certain 'things', forms of mechanisation, and so forth, our efforts will be in vain. Indeed, Adorno firmly states in many passages in his work, 'there is no substratum beneath such "deformations", no ontic interior on which social mechanisms merely act externally'.[68] There is nothing originary, everything is always mediated.

He blocks the way to this interpretation at three different levels, by refuting the normativity of any supposed anthropological depths; by challenging the idea of natural determination in the biological sense; and by denying all reality to a core of individual identity.

Adorno provides, notably in *Negative Dialectics*, a clear-cut critique of the idea of self-alienation, which wrongly implies that, prior to the advent of capitalism and the alienation it engenders, human beings had simply been themselves, or had been able to realise their humanity. He pays tribute to Marx's late writing for dispensing with the fantasy of an era that would have been free from corruption and yet for remaining faithful to the idea that the process of capitalist production transforms human beings into mere appendages of the machine.[69] Conversely, he took a distance from Lukács for similar reasons: 'The meaningful times for whose return the early Lukács yearned were as much due to reification, to inhuman institutions, as he would later attest it only to the bourgeois age.'[70]

The undistorted essence presumed by the notion of alienation or self-alienation does not exist; human beings have never simply been themselves. The substantial element, to which it is a question of being faithful, or of hoping that it is possible to be faithful in order to confer dignity on one's person, does not exist. The concept of man itself is a mystification, a poor determination that cannot be erected as a rampart against injustice and with which one cannot 'push the gate opening the domain of the essence'.[71]

Neither is there any natural determination to be discovered. The biological, or the living, does not come to replace being in so far as it is endowed with a project.

As Adorno writes in a letter to Benjamin, and more precisely in an unkind passage dedicated to Caillois, it is crucial that 'the reified separation of spheres like the biological on one side and the socio-historical on the other' 'be exploded'.[72] This implies integrating historical dynamics into biology, and biology into historical dynamics. For him, the biological given is continuously determined and elaborated by a cultural practice. And as Bernstein[73] points out, there is no way of knowing what we have lost during the process of development of reason and domination of nature – including internal nature. What we are is the result of this process of domination.

In particular, Adorno applies this reasoning to the idea of 'need', a category as necessary as it is suspect *qua* object of the social sciences and basis for normative reasoning. For him, need is a social category. There is something about it that pertains to nature, 'But the social and natural moments of need cannot be split up into secondary and primary in order to set up some sort of ranking of satisfactions.'[74] Distinguishing between 'true' and 'false' needs on this basis is therefore illusory.

In the same way, it is impossible to isolate something like a *raw* impulse that, *as such*, would make me attentive to the other, and from which I could be alienated. Every drive is socially mediated. The idea of a supplement (*Hinzutrende*), the aforementioned instance that 'precedes the ego',[75] that is a moral impulse both somatic and intra-mental, works precisely to challenge the idea of a pure biological datum that we would 'run into'. At the same time, it averts the pitfall of an impulse that being natural is immutable, and which would be the basis for a determination of essence with the value of a primary principle. Above all, as already mentioned, it is the *history* of the West, its derailment towards Auschwitz, which has made the body the last resort for a life lived less wrongly.

As early as his 1932 lecture on the idea of natural history, Adorno states that the relationship between nature and history can only be grasped 'if it is possible to comprehend historical being in its most extreme historical determinacy, where it is most historical, as natural being; or if it were possible to comprehend nature as an historical being, where it seems to rest most deeply in itself as nature'.[76] Each of the two concepts of history and nature can therefore only be mobilised in a critical function vis-à-vis the other.

The reconciliation with nature that Adorno so desires in no way implies a 'return' to it. By contrast, it requires individuals, on the one hand, to reflect on themselves in their quality as elements of nature (the fact that they are bodies, but also the fact that they are part of nature in their compulsive attempt to master it[77]) and, on the other, to reach a higher degree of autonomy from it. 'To free' nature – internal as well as external – is certainly not Adorno's project. If he frequently denounces the repression of nature, it is not because it has lost its immediacy, its originarity, but because it has been mediated and used in the wrong way (by being constituted as the other of culture).

In his opinion, the nature argument is always a powerful tool of domination; to appeal to nature 'is always merely the mask of denial and domination'.[78] A perfect, and ironic, illustration of the enchantment delivered by the idea of nature is also at the core of the exchange form. Since, as with Marx, for whom fetishism is the naturalisation of a historical relationship, and in the very first place of commercial exchange, Adorno considers that, 'Without disregard for living human beings there could be no exchange. What this implies in the real progress of life to this day is the necessity of social semblance. Its core is value as a thing-in-itself, value as "nature".'[79]

Finally, there can be no return to an authentic core of the self at the end of a reflexive process or as a result of a shock, because no such core exists. Interiority is as inextricable from the effects of socialisation and domination as nature; it is as unlikely a candidate for the status of a substrate exposed to an external threat as anthropology.

There is no place in Adorno's thought for a conception of individual identity that this individual owes itself to recover, for a call to some fidelity to its own foundation, for the designation of the possible place of a buried integrity towards which it should forge a path. Far from embracing the 'heroic endurance of an individual existence "thrown into the world"',[80] Adorno argues that the evocation of authenticity, such as it is found in Søren Kierkegaard or Martin Heidegger in particular, only protects the existing order. Because it contains an absolute conception of the substantiality of the self, the idea of authenticity is an imposture; because its call to choose oneself seems to be situated at a philosophical level, it conceals the social origin of the individual's title to property with respect to itself;[81] and because it calls for a withdrawal, for one to become harder, it is nothing other than 'the stubborn, obstinate insistence on the monadic form that social oppression imposes on men'.[82]

Adorno's reflections on the theme of authenticity block in advance the way for Honneth's argument according to which Adorno entertains a fascination for childhood as a moment of unmediated contact with an always-already moral interiority that is then forgotten: 'It is precisely undeviating self-reflection – the practice of which Nietzsche called psychology, that is, insistence on the truth about oneself, that shows again and again, even in the first conscious experiences of childhood, that the impulses reflected upon are not quite "genuine".'[83]

We might rather interpret the thesis of forgetting as follows: Adorno's concern is that the conditions for the development of solidarity, defined as solidarity with other 'torturable bodies', the injunction of which is to cease all physical suffering, are not given in the absence of institutions to support moral life in an appropriate way. Our social context generates bourgeois coldness not by suffocating what would have been there in all other circumstances, but by constituting a wrong, bad (*falsch*) second nature (if we conceive the 'first' nature as that of biology and physics). The human 'nature' produced by the historical process and the practical activity proper to capitalist society does not enclose a concern leading one to feel responsible for others but, on the contrary, leads to indifference. What is more, this indifference erases its social texture by cloaking itself in the attributes of naturalness.

On this reading, which I am defending here, the problem of the second nature that is coldness is not that it breaks and corrupts the first nature, because nothing indicates there is any preceding reality. Just as it is not necessary, according to Adorno, to know right in order to perceive wrong, nor is it necessary to know what a human being is, or even should be, to determine 'what he should not be and what configuration of human affairs is wrong'.[84]

Rather than suffocating, neutralising, atrophying or suppressing moral dispositions or competences, they must instead be thought of as being *rendered impossible*. This interpretation is confirmed by another of Adorno's reflections, this time the psychoanalytically inflected discussion on the prevention of more deliberative and rational forms of concern for others, which is to say of the 'individual' as the moment of constitution of the human being's moral autonomy.

The individual cannot be understood, in its features and faculties, in particular moral, separately from the institution of the bourgeois family. In the late 1930s Adorno and Horkheimer sought to diagnose the decline of the bourgeois and patriarchal family under the effects of rationalisation and the logic of generalised domination. According to them, the result was the constitution of a 'new type of man',[85] one that operates in the conditions of monopolistic capitalism and is produced by direct and immediate state-led socialisation.

The new humans manufactured in this post-family era are not individuals: at the same time as the continuity of experience is broken, the self as an instance disappears. This disappearance opens the way to the constitution of collective subjects, while weak individualities seek to overcome their powerlessness by becoming part of the masses and conditioned by their affects. This new socialisation no longer allows the construction of psychological and moral autonomy. Adorno and Horkheimer indeed follow Freud in his conviction that it is bourgeois paternal authority that creates individuals endowed with a moral autonomy via the Oedipus complex, which is at the origin of the constitution of the superego.[86]

Reasoned concern for others is therefore prevented by the generalisation of an authoritarian character that predisposes one to conformism, to a 'conventionalism' that dismisses any temptation to deliberate morally, to reflect properly on what is due to others. This is a phenomenon that Nazism brought to its apogee. Nazism deprives moral consciousness of any object, because the individual's sense of responsibility towards him- or herself and others becomes replaced by their contribution to the machinery.[87] Under such conditions, it is no longer possible for one to perceive one's share of guilt, because social imperatives are no longer internalised in a way that confers them a strong obligatory character that enables society to be emancipated by their being turned against society; all that is now produced is direct identification with hierarchical scales of stereotyped values.

If this thesis is problematic from a gender perspective owing to the idealisation of the bourgeois family it conveys – a point to which I return below – it nevertheless points to two successive bases of subjectivation, namely the family and the market (organised by the state). It provides some indications about what Adorno called the market formation of 'not only professional, but *anthropological* types', or 'specific substances',[88] of human beings suited to the market's different forms and phases. The market does not stifle a natural competence which the family has allowed to blossom. Instead, these two mechanisms give rise to different moral subjectivations, with the former leaving *little*, and the latter *no*, room for concern for others.

Hence, the thesis of forgetting does not implicitly forge the motif of a competence that is already there and that capitalism alters or simply extinguishes. Rather, it refers to a disposition pertaining to a second nature, which is to neglect what we know. Jessica Benjamin's psychoanalytically inspired argument has it that Adorno's originality lies in the idea that domination does not work by repressing instincts but by repressing what is *already known*, and specifically the awareness that one has of one's own impotence and complicity with the powerful, the knowledge that one holds of the profound fictiveness of the 'individual'.[89] Similarly, it seems to me possible to argue that the perception, which indeed takes place, of all an object's aspects, of all the possibles of a reality, of the distress of others, is *struck off as irrelevant*, as is the horizon of obligations, responsibilities and doubts that would unfold if we did not forget this perception. There is no faculty that is unlearned or deinstalled. To forget does not mean not to have a memory of something. It means denying all causal power, all aptness, all authority to certain of the lived experiences, especially painful ones, and properties of others. To use Benjamin's expression to define aura, it means not allowing such properties and lived experiences the power to 'make one look up'. Ignoring the links that these properties and lived experiences have with the rest of the world, including with ourselves, we are able to erase all that we owe them with respect to concern.

Moreover, *Dialectics of Enlightenment* thematises forgetting in a parallel with anaesthesia, as Adorno and Horkheimer reprise the now discarded argument that the sleeping patient, far from feeling no pain, only forgets it when they wake up. To forget therefore means to sever all continuity and attachment with the moment or content of the lived experience of suffering – own's one suffering and that of others – that we have *nevertheless* perceived or felt. And this occultation affects our present relationship to others and to ourselves as much as it affects our common and personal future, since the ability to experience the new depends on a form of memory, of fidelity: 'it is only by keeping up certain thoughts to the point at which they invert that certain new experiences can become possible'.[90]

This thesis of forgetting, and the diagnosis of the coldness it accompanies, bears on a generalised process that affects all human beings without distinction within the capitalist form of life; it applies to the bourgeoisie as well as to workers, to intellectuals as well as to those who only consume the products of the culture industry, and – here I come to the core of my concern – to men as well as to women.

3 A Forgetting in the Thesis of Forgetting

In *Critical Models*, there is a very preliminary mention of a model of education by hardness, one founded on an identification of virility and the ability to endure. To be a man, one must be trained to be hard, which is to say 'absolutely indifferent toward pain as such. In this the distinction between one's own pain and that of another is not so stringently maintained.'[1] This brief evocation aside, Adorno grasps the rendering impossible of concern for others without considering the order of gender. His reading is, however, bluntly belied by women's experience and carrying out of care as something that serves both the reproduction of capitalist society and the coldness that accompanies and generalises exchange. The Adornian thesis of forgetting would thus seem to conceal a forgetting – namely that of a specificity imparted to women in the moral economy of the capitalist form of life.

It indeed appears necessary to take into consideration the fact that within capitalism sectors or practices that escape the market coexist with sectors or practices woven by the market, and that capitalism is based on *both* kinds of arrangement. Many Marxist feminists have investigated not only what Marx called the 'secret abode of production', but also its backstory,[2] and revealed that one condition of the market is notably the possibility that there are social relationships which remain foreign to it. Among these, and sustaining or replenishing them, are what has been called care, affective labour, social reproduction. The market not only feeds on the resources it finds in its environment, especially moral ones, to ensure the maintenance of social bonds on the one hand and the production and care of embodied and needy human beings on the other; the market also releases waste back into this same environment – not only industrial waste into nature, but also 'human waste' into the family, such as the sick, disabled persons and the elderly, and thereby depends on that which remains foreign to it.[3]

It is the inherently gendered aspects of the market's conditions of possibility and the modalities of Adorno's avoidance of them that must now be explored. I will therefore delve into his remarks on 'woman', before shining the raw light supplied by theories of care on a blind spot in his theory of concern for others – its gendered distribution. I then go on to establish the relevance that bringing these two theoretical corpuses head to head has for our understanding of contemporary capitalism, which is no longer the capitalism that Adorno had observed.

Adorno and 'Woman'

In Adorno's work women are generally presented as objects of caricatured determinations, figuring under pathetic and obligatory figures such as 'the' shrew, 'the' virgin, 'the' *bayadère*, 'the' wife and so on, all of which together make up 'woman'. What is more, however, Adorno enumerates multiple stereotypes which he invests with truth. Accordingly, 'woman' is said to demonstrate a fascination for the esoteric, notably linked to the fact that 'she feels herself drawn to mischief'.[4] She is said to be as irreducibly docile as she is captivated by the norm ('without a single exception feminine natures are conformist'[5]). And her behaviour towards commodities, clothes as much as hairstyles, is alleged to be completely irrational.[6]

These statements do not come in for denunciation; Adorno deems them to be true in that they describe the administered world, the world of mass production in which 'stereotypes replace intellectual categories'.[7] From there the glorification of the feminine character, which consists of a collage of clichés that also contain features at first sight positive, such as an affinity with beauty and its culture, 'implies the humiliation of all who bear it'.[8]

Backdropped by such vignettes, Adorno mounts a series of odd, unsound arguments about women and the gender order that we must now unfold in their complexity.

Adorno on the Gender Order: Shadows Cast and Light Shed

It is easy to demonstrate that Adorno's conception of the bourgeois family, observed from the point of view of its decline, carries an implicit patriarchal normativity. Jessica Benjamin has thus highlighted some problematic assumptions contained in Adorno and Horkheimer's account of the decline of the individual. The importance that both give to overcoming narcissism in defining moral autonomy, that is the idea that a distant but idealised father, representing external authorities, is introduced into the ego ideal, is deeply gendered; it considers only the position of the son who identifies with his father. Moreover, masculinity, like the autonomy to which it is connected, is thus defined on the basis of the child's necessary tearing away from the dyad he forms with his mother. Such an idea denies the possibility of a maternal education able to foster autonomy. Finally, because freedom presupposes the internalisation of a pre-existing authority, the adult capacity to resist requires strong paternal figures in order to defeat them. Adorno describes, and rues, the advent of a 'fatherless society', to borrow Jessica Benjamin's expression.[9]

The passages that Adorno devotes to the bourgeois family are more widely permeated with nostalgia, since this family represents for him the mode of socialisation prior to barbarism. Thus, in an aphorism bearing on parents in general, we read the following:

> With the family there passes away, while the system lasts, not only the most effective agency of the bourgeoisie, but also the resistance which, though repressing the individual, also strengthened perhaps even produced him. The end of the family paralyses the forces of opposition.[10]

This nostalgia is not embarrassed by the fact that, for women, the dissolution of this family unit, as Adorno himself describes it in its function of production and sustaining of a human subject suitable for capitalism – a function to which women in particular were assigned – did not in any way constitute a loss.

There are, however, also passages in which Adorno takes up feminist concerns.

The 'entry' of women into the labour market is described as a ruse of domination. Seemingly empowering, this move only completes women's integration into the administered world and increases their subjugation: 'The admittance of women to every conceivable supervised activity conceals continuing dehumanization. In big business they remain what they were in the family, objects.'[11]

It is notably in *Minima Moralia* where he states the political coordinates of his stance: 'The feminine character is a negative imprint of domination. But therefore equally bad.'[12] This is because female subjectivity is partially removed from the system of power, in so far as it is the incomplete – one could almost say failed – product of reason's expansion through its logic of domination of nature. This subjectivity does not, however, constitute a possible site of resistance. There is no truth in a feminine path or voice. Female experience and subjectivity escape absolute domination, not in the sense of constituting a plane of reality in which the possibility of emancipation is sedimented, but in the sense of appearing as a *trace*, almost as a *scar* left by nature on the human race. 'Woman' gives us a glimpse of non-dominated nature, because nature imprints a difference on her (she is 'smaller and weaker'). Which is surely the most 'shaming' thing possible in a virile society.[13] But it is also an indelible mark of nature. In this way, women are associated with the theme of reminiscence and recollection: they prevent us from forgetting that of which they bear the trace. They excite nostalgia for a form of life that does not coincide with the domination of nature, and with it the memory of the suffering endured by everyone in the course of the unfolding of the reign of reason. Here, in reverse, we find the reason for forgetting as a necessary mechanism for domination. This pitiful form of opposition to the forgetting that women represent at the level of their bodies shows the failure of the power system to effect total closure, yet without offering any prospect for its overthrow.

In Adorno's writings, 'woman' is also regularly associated with a powerlessness inherent in her inability to defend herself, which thus 'sort of legitimizes her oppression',[14] but also with a powerlessness which essentially pertains to all human beings in the administered world. This latter powerlessness is brought to such a level of evidence in women that, unable to hide it, those who look at women are forced to see the vanity of their own feelings of power, based as they are on the sole, and falsely emancipatory, subjection of nature.[15] The woman forces one to contemplate one's own helplessness.

The motif of the resentment to which the 'woman' gives rise crops up as insistently as the foregoing themes, and is contiguous to them. The disfigured face that 'she' presents because she is marked by a lack of mastery of things arouses animosity and rancour. The special status granted to her as compensation has the same effect: ideologically compensating women's oppression with respect for them has only created a rancour against the woman thus sublimated. Moreover, as I mentioned at the start of this book, for Adorno and Horkheimer, nature, which is perceived as weakness and fragility, gives rise to a sadistic impulse which increases as instrumental reason becomes more totalised. Similar to external nature, the body is a possible, necessary object of brutality. In this invitation to violence the Christian humiliation of the flesh converges with the secular association of the exploited body with evil (spirit gleans the supreme good), an association performed even by the exploited themselves. The conspicuous body of woman then comes in for a particular violence.

Nevertheless, these apparently feminist passages are precisely where Adorno's most reactionary positions on male–female relations emerge. Many aspects of his critique of patriarchy are highly problematic since the critique itself is based on the conviction that women 'have no autonomous share in the capabilities which gave rise to this civilization. The man must go out into hostile life, must act and strive. The woman is not a subject. *She does not produce anything* but looks after the producers.'[16] The distinction between production and reproduction, classically Marxist, and classically blind to the fact that reproduction also constitutes work and is part of the 'capabilities which gave rise to this civilization', is in his view the place for a fragmentary reflection on women's *own* subjection to the exchange form.

In a letter to Erich Fromm dated 16 November 1937, a copy of which was addressed to Horkheimer, Adorno presented an outline for a never-implemented project on 'the feminine character'[17] which was to be part of a series of empirical works for the Institut für Sozialforschung. His aim was to establish this 'character' based on Marx's analysis of the commodity form. Once again, the issue was to avoid any psychologising of the phenomenon, or use of explanatory categories such as internalisation; Adorno wanted a diagnosis based solely on an objective position in an economy where what is key is the form. Departing from Freud, he refuted the latter's theory that women are conditioned through their identification with men:

I think that we can avoid resorting to the mechanism of identification, which would be very difficult to prove anyway, if we succeed in directly reducing female psychology to the position of women within the production and consumption process. Identification with man probably only occurs in a roundabout way, through the use of goods whose idolatry seems to me to be the key factor.[18]

He discovered with measured enthusiasm that Leo Löwenthal's article on Ibsen provided the sketch of just such a 'character', a sketch, in keeping with his own project, based on the premise that women do not participate in the process of economic production. The problem is that, according to Adorno's reading of it in his letter to Fromm, Löwenthal attributes a lower degree of reification, a less mutilated sexuality and weaker repression to women than to men, a conclusion that Adorno describes as romantic. For him, on the contrary, 'women are more dominated by the commodity character than are men';[19] riveted to consumption, they function as the agents of commodities in society. The woman even relates to her own body as a commodity. She is therefore always-already commensurable, she 'forgets' herself to consider those aspects and possibilities of herself that exceed her status as a commodity. The conviction that women are external to the sphere of production is an idea that Adorno still found convincing almost twenty years later in Thorstein Veblen's work, which, in *Prisms*, he also fiercely criticises: according to Veblen, being exempted from 'practical life' because of her degrading situation as an object of ostentation, woman is not forced to develop the predatory spirit required by competition; for this reason she retains 'aptitudes in which a humanity survives'.[20] But what interests Adorno, in terms that he admits to be an overinterpretation of Veblen, is that 'women have escaped the sphere of production only to be absorbed all the more entirely by the sphere of consumption, to be captivated by the immediacy of the commodity'.[21]

This means that if, as we saw in the previous chapter, capitalism is defined for Adorno primarily by exchange, rather than by production or exploitation, women then find themselves at the very heart of capital's endless expansion. This is *not* so, however, by virtue of their attention to others and the unpaid or low-paid work in which they engage. Their role involves a particular investment of exchange value, a specific activation of the commodity form that shapes even their bodies, a specific and exacerbated fetishism.

That is why they do not escape the system of domination in any way; it is others, men, discourses, objects in so far as they embody myth, that project this illusion on them and their bodies. They remain external to the system as signs, brands; as subjects they are an essential part of its machinery.

Adorno also advances the idea that because of women's specific position in relation to production, the construction of the ego of most of them remains incomplete. They manifest a stronger infantilism than men; at the same time, they in no way prove to be more progressive than men. He therefore discloses some specifically female traits based on an analysis of the position of women in the economy, his intention being to show how these traits serve the perpetuation of society and, more radically still, how they 'lead to the fascist reproduction of stupidity'.[22]

This shift towards the theme of fascism adds a moral dimension to Adorno's investigation, and reintroduces, along with the enthusiastic bowing down before power with which fascism coincides, the question of coldness.

Indeed, if we look closely, the diagnosing of all human beings as having a radical indifference to others is not only implicit. If women are not named, it is because they, too, like men, are prey to phenomena of phantasmagoria, of submission to self-preservation, of the impoverishing of experience, and so on. Indeed, for Adorno, they embody a particular mode of unaffection.

Cold, Furiously Cold Women

The women featuring in Adorno's highly caricatured sketches almost always stand out for their almost jubilant indifference. They engage in a disengaged observation of the suffering of others, they demonstrate an inability, or unwillingness, to put themselves in the place of others, they eagerly subscribe to the inevitable, and so forth, but this coldness proves less objective, or rather more subjectively invested, than it does when Adorno describes coldness as a universal phenomenon, that is as carved out with regard to masculine roles. Here the effects of generalised commensurability remain in the background, while he shows us the multiple ways in which coldness has crept into the smallest folds of feminine subjectivity.

For what singularises such subjectivity is certainly not a privileged relationship to love. The wife and the prostitute, both established, fairly conventionally, as complementary faces of female alienation in the patriarchal world, decline this complementarity in their complete absence of concern for men. Both are described as engaged in an undertaking to prevent male pleasure: 'the wife betrays pleasure to the fixed order of life and property, while the harlot, as her secret accomplice, brings within the property relationship that which the wife's property rights do not include – pleasure – by selling it.'[23]

The improbability of their gift-giving excludes *a fortiori* the possibility of self-giving. There is no place in the female subject sketched by Adorno for the vulnerability of the moral agent that care theories frequently evoke, which is related to the propensity for self-sacrifice, to the possibility of forgetting and of pouring oneself into endless and limitless caregiving.[24] Adorno states, on the contrary, that 'women with their archaic fear are just as incapable as men with their self-importance'[25] of that unending willingness for self-abandonment. Far from developing a propensity for unending devotion, women display behaviours that are as much shaped by the primacy of self-preservation as those of men – all that varies is the psychological mechanism of its deployment. With women this mechanism concerns fear, which stimulates an exclusive concern for the survival and preservation of immediate interests, the driving force behind their indifference to all that is foreign to them.

Moreover, coldness additionally densifies, including in its feminine forms, as capitalism develops. Adorno tells us that there is nothing left of the solicitude or solidarity that bourgeois women might still have shown in Ibsen's time towards their hysterical sisters, that is towards those who attempted to escape the prison of their lives. 'Their granddaughters, however, would smile indulgently over these hysterics, without even feeling implicated, and hand them over to the benevolent treatment of social welfare.'[26] Adorno does not go as far as Horkheimer, who thematises the universal expunging of concern for others as being *specific* to late capitalism, which he alleges has replaced an earlier gendered differentiation. Horkheimer indeed diagnoses a decline in maternal care, which he attributes to the professionalisation of motherhood, that is, its standardisation according to new principles of social hygiene and efficiency. The introduction of child education and media discourse, as well as the 'emotional coldness' of mothers who now work out of home, all lead to a lack of real emotional relationships between mother and child. According to Horkheimer, it is only in the very last phase of capitalism that indifference also becomes feminine.[27] For Adorno, however, there is no discernible historical rupture; instead, we bear witness only to a process by which the rendering impossible of all moral dispositions becomes increasingly certain.

In one of his few empirical studies, he gives a list of the characteristics which point to a strong susceptibility to being seduced by fascism, notably including a lack of pity for the poor. It is only under this aspect of the 'authoritarian personality' that a gendered variable is introduced:[28] women, he notes, share this tendency less, by channelling it into social assistance and charity. No concern for others is implied here, however. For it is through charity that the woman 'humiliates the one she claims to help, and [. . .] in reality does not help anyone but only takes advantage of it to feel important'.[29]

That woman's disposition to care for others is struck with impossibility is evinced as radically as possible in pogroms, in which, Adorno tells us, her 'bloodthirstiness' eclipses that of men.[30] Her responsibility for Nazism is the same as that of men, her objective powerlessness does not exempt her from the 'nexus of complicity' (Schuldzusammenhang) [31] mentioned in the first chapter. We are far from Luce Irigaray's proclaiming: 'We should not tolerate that our mothers are accused of being a pillar of fascism! Were they in power? Did they have any say in the choice of plan?'[32] For Adorno, *because* they are unable to change the world, women *participate* in the evil that it constitutes. There is more, however: their powerlessness leads them to outdo men and their indifference; women put real rage into their hardness.

It remains to consider the few passages in which Adorno does seem to adopt the idea of a specifically feminine concern for others, as when in the notes and sketches that complete *Dialectic of Enlightenment* he observes, with Horkheimer, that concern for animals has been left by Western civilisation to women, and that the bourgeoisie more broadly draws benefit from feminine virtue and morality. But Adorno does not emend the 'forgetting' in his thesis about forgetting, which is the specificity imparted to women by the moral economy of the capitalist form of life. Female virtue and morality are described as the products of 'reaction formations of the matriarchal rebellion',[33] simply instrumentalised by capitalist society. They are foreign bodies to the capitalist organisation of work, tolerated and to some extent opportunely called upon. The evocation of prehistoric matriarchal periods is certainly very problematic, the seeming suggestion being that, unlike men who have never been themselves, women once enjoyed an era before their disfigurement, a 'maenadic' past. However, this passage clearly indicates that gender-based difference in the distribution of virtue and attention to others is not an effect of capitalism. Above all, the rest of the text teaches us what remains of a concern for others: the solidarity of which the woman is still capable with 'creatures' is expressed nowhere more than in her passion for the Pekinese.[34] The share of solicitude that seems to be left to women is only a mimicry, a mere rictus.

Accordingly, Adorno traces a general neutralisation of moral dispositions, wherein gender – whose order is the focus of an accurate reflection in his work – produces only variants of coldness. The meagre difference between men and women results on the one hand from the particular integration of women into the capitalist system, which proceeds through exchange rather than production, and on the other hand from a subjective investment more or less marked by indifference to others.

Gendered Moral Dispositions: A Reading of Care Theories

Lying at the heart of the thinking of many theorists of care is the conviction that the always-already gendered distribution of care work is based on a gendered distribution of concern for others. [35]

Joan Tronto, in particular, has argued that the activity of care ought not to be grasped through the prism of a dyad formed by the caregiver and the care receiver. She urges us instead to take into consideration the way in which, when this dyad materialises, it is actually set within a general organisation of work, both concrete and moral, composed of all those who participate as well as all those who do not participate in this activity, one that includes, as aforementioned, 'everything that we do to maintain, continue, and repair our "world" so that we can live in it as well as possible'.[36] This dyad presupposes, among other things, a general economy of affects; the moral dispositions themselves are differentially allocated by certain structures of domination. The ability to respond to and perceive vulnerability, far from being a matter of inherent sensitivity or irrepressible emotional reactions, comes about through the organisation of the social.

The fact that some – mostly male subjects – harbour a tendency to exempt themselves from certain responsibilities, and others – mostly female subjects – a certainty that situations of dependence or fragility leave them no choice but to respond, stems from a multitude of structures underpinning male domination: ideological constructions, gender-role sedimentation, biographical scripts, the incorporation of social structures, phantasmagoria of romantic love, and so forth, which accumulate without really clashing.

Self-esteem is thus a powerful motivational force leading to the voluntary assumption of tasks and duties which serve the gendered societal order. Self-realisation thus depends, for some, on maintaining a fidelity to certain moral feelings. Carol Gilligan has demonstrated that, 'Although independent assertion in judgment and action is considered to be the hallmark of adulthood, it is rather in their care and concern for others that women have both judged themselves and been judged.'[37] She thus suggests that the division of labour is secured, even more than by the injunction to identity based on a threat of social sanction, by the promise of a relationship with oneself that is not painful.

In the professional context, the idea of vocation also effectively covers over the effective allocation of responsibilities, in so far as precedence is assigned to the subject over the work he or she does. Some are allegedly gifted for certain tasks, certain forms of devotion, and correlatively have a calling for them, while others do not.[38]

The emergence of a feminine concern for others is also served by certain biographical events. Penelope Deutscher has drawn attention to the very particular site of reproductive choices as a key part of the gendered manufacturing of certain moral dispositions. Deutscher gives a reading of the interviews that Gilligan conducted in *A Different Voice*, which, as she observed women facing the possibility of having an abortion, permitted her to shape the contours of her ethic of care. Deutscher shows that the decision about whether to continue or to terminate a pregnancy is a site of normalisation of the female moral subject, and that this normalisation rests on submitting to the imperative of a certain complexity in emotional life.[39] Facing a reproductive choice for women means being placed in circumstances in which it is expected that they will adopt an introspective posture, engage in moral reflection and undergo powerful emotions. Interactions with health professionals, psychologists, but also with peers or the media contribute to shaping a psychological interiority that comes to be seen as *the sign* of the existence of a moral subject. In this sense, advice and introspection thus constitute technologies of subjectivation. Producing a psychological state character-ised by its depth, they also concretise the responsibility that is at the heart of an ethic of care. The moral subjectification of women itself coincides here with the ability to demonstrate and feel a concern for others. In the absence of this attention to others, of the contextualised consideration it implies, of the enunciation of an emotionally charged narrative, women quite simply are not seen as moral subjects.

Some theorists of care have also pointed out that knowl-edge of and attention to vulnerability do not necessarily precede the act of caring for it. The act also produces such knowledge and attention as an outcome, which is why con-cern for others is the prerogative of those who are assigned to care work. Care activities thus generate the sensitivity they require: concern for others arises from the practical activity of caring for their needs. According to Sandra Laugier's ver-sion of this approach, there is a specific economy of attention in each society, such that phenomena of invisibility (e.g. the existence of distress or need of some sort) must be under-stood less as the effect of an ideological veil than as the result of a quotidian inattention. Neglected realities are not neces-sarily hidden; they can also be 'already in front of us, spread out before our eyes',[40] and not figured as part of *what matters*. Overcoming these imperceptibilities, then, requires specific attention to the non-visible greatness of things and people, to the burying of important things in our everyday lives. Daily contact with that which does not matter sharpens a particular attention, and a concern, for it.

The modalities of the gendered distribution of solicitude may be further specified through a reflection on the existence of 'feeling rules', that is, on social expectations towards feel-ings related to a conventional definition of a situation, which

Arlie Hochschild highlights in her book *The Managed Heart*. Hochschild points out that individuals are capable of emotional work, performed by modifying the degree or quality of their feelings in response to an obligation to adjust their feelings to a situation. These feeling rules vary depending on the social group in question.[41] Correlatively, Hochschild demonstrates how empathetic employee–customer interactions are produced through certain forms of organisation of work. As she sees it, contemporary capitalism is far from making subjects 'forget' empathy and much more about subjecting its uses to multiple forms of instrumentalisation[42] through steering the emotional labour of employees. While in certain occupations such labour is carried out by both men and women (the supporting empirical research comprises interviews with airline flight attendants), it is far more frequent and concentrated among women, particularly because, as Hochschild maintains, women tend to use their feelings as resources to the extent they are deprived of other types of capital, symbolic or material. The link between gendered emotional structuring and domination is further strengthened by women's specialisation in the sort of emotional work that affirms, enhances and celebrates the well-being and status of others. Bringing this demonstration into the conceptual framework of an ethic of care makes it possible to show how emotional work also underlies the unpaid activities assigned to women, and more broadly the fulfilling of expectations for roles shouldered by women in terms of solicitude and attention to the needs of others, thus reinforcing, directing or even fostering some of their moral dispositions.[43]

Finally, some have drawn attention to the role of concern for others as part of the *mechanism* of gender domination, where concern is not only the trace or the result of this domination but also reinforces and relays it. Nel Noddings has thus insisted on the caregiver's own vulnerability to the person she is caring for from the moment she is truly committed to ensuring this person's well-being. One who recognises the ethical value of care, and chooses to live in accordance with it, experiences this responsibility as really crushing;[44] care work, which deeply structures one's relationship to the world and all those one does not have to take care of, brings with it a heavy psychological burden, reducing the horizon of possibilities as much as the capacity for action. Accordingly, Dietmut Bubeck insists that only by considering the caregiver's receptiveness to the other's emotional texture can we account for the structural possibility of her exploitation. This concern is precisely what makes it impossible to abandon a task or even to distance oneself from a person; it is what makes it difficult to start a conflict. And the problem is all the more acute because it is a type of commitment that care providers themselves acknowledge as part of their work.[45] In other words, gender-differentiated moral dispositions can transform emotional vulnerability into a structural social handicap as well as make these women vulnerable to exploitation or 'labour extortion'.[46]

The fragility of concern for others, or 'coldness', to reprise the Adornian notion, as that which characterises the male role, is not a topic that theories of care have fleshed out or developed to the same extent. Such theories mainly explain coldness away as the 'the irresponsibility of the privileged' or 'the indifference of the privileged'.[47] Joan Tronto remarks that not being assigned any responsibilities in a given society's distribution of them will occur for one of two reasons: the first results from phenomena of exclusion (some are unable to participate in this distribution, are a priori excluded from it); the second, less frequently analysed, option is the possibility of exempting oneself from this participation, which she calls 'privileged irresponsibility'.[48] The latter concerns the fact that some people grant themselves the right not to perform certain tasks, owing not to some unjustifiable privilege but claiming that they have other social responsibilities. The absence or inoperability of certain moral dispositions is therefore interpreted less in terms of the incorporation of a virility that would pass through a prohibition of moral emotions than as a negligence that is couched in terms of freedom, as a possibility for some to neglect types of hardship with which they are not confronted.

And by systematically delegating care activities and their accompanying attitudes to women (and other subordinate groups), members of the dominant groups can, by exempting themselves from such activities, entertain the fiction of their independence, which in turn contributes to maintaining relations of domination by fuelling invisibility or maintaining the illusion that care needs are exceptional.[49]

What is suggested by this exercise of conjoint discussion between Adorno's reflection and ethical theories of care is a conception of the fragility of moral dispositions not as a generalised and levelling exposure to a risk of 'forgetting', but instead as a social distribution both of 'forgetting' of dispositions and of the dispositions themselves – or some of them. By bringing these theories head to head, we are led to the idea of gender-differentiated *subjectivations*, radically distinct from any representation of graduated processes which neutralise supposedly pregiven moral emotions. We must thus be careful, however, not to conceive of two sorts of subjectivation that occur in parallel and as the inversion of one another: admirable women and blameworthy men. The challenge is rather to consider how, within a form of life that ingrains indifference across the board, women are imparted a compartmentalised attention to others, limited to modes and fields apt to producing particular forms of labour or consumption. But in order to advance this argument it is necessary to verify the acuity of the tools used for thinking about the contemporary era. Indeed, recent changes in capitalism, such as those in the organisation of care activities, may well have rendered this essay's two theoretical resources redundant.

Coldness and Concern for Others after Late Capitalism

In response to the 'crisis' of care, there are several ongoing tendencies in the way that care is being organised in the West. Care is undergoing commercialisation (its devolution to the market), a return to the familial fold, and subsequent com-modification (for example, through regulations on the pos-sibility of remunerating family carers). It is also caught up in successive games of removing from and reintroducing into the public domain certain tasks of care and education. These pro-cesses of reorganisation do not disturb the gender boundaries, however. For households they often entail complex arrange-ments around paid and unpaid work, but they always call for a 'primary caregiver' who, in the overwhelming majority of cases, is a woman. [50]

Sociological studies have closely documented men's ongo-ing lack of investment in domestic work,[51] which is perhaps the only aspect of gender inequalities where an almost absolute absence of change is observable. And while not all women are now assigned these activities, responsibilities for them come to be 'distributed among women hierarchically'.[52]

This continued difference between men and women involves more than care as labour. Caroline Ibos's ethnographic survey of a group of nannies and their employers in Paris thus highlights how the relationship that is most often forged in the domestic space is one between two women – the nanny and her female employer – from which the male spouse is wholly exempt. It is generally only the female employer who forges the potentially difficult and conflictual relationship with the couple's employee. On the one hand, it follows from this three-way relationship, whose female partners are the only true actors, that the male spouse's social status and career – which depends on his professional availability, the exemplarity of his children's behaviour, and the attractiveness of his apartment – hinges on the labour of the two women.[53] On the other hand, having a concern for others remains, in terms of the issues, inconveniences and ambiguities that it raises, a largely feminine matter. Indeed, it is generally the female employer alone who tackles issues to do with which deeds to perform or words to use to help maintain a shared understanding within a relationship that is socially unequal and, due to the post-colonial context, often historically charged.

The problem of the possible out-of-dateness of Adorno's theory of capitalism must also be examined and calls for a more complex response. Changes and ruptures, reflected in expressions such as neo-capitalism, post-Fordist capitalism, the third age of capitalism, and so forth, have undeniably taken place since the 1960s. In addition to the fact that the idea of bureaucratic planning, and more broadly the place conferred by Adorno on the state in the functioning of capitalism, seem completely outdated, we can mention the decline of industrial production (at least in the western world), the emergence of new information technologies and the digital revolution, but also the financialisation of capital and the dynamic of privatising and commercialising what had till then been considered a public good, as factors that mark a new stage in the commodification of the world. All this has resulted in profound transformations in how work is organised, in a mutation of management structures, and an upheaval within waged labour (for example, by dissolving the limits of the working day), transformations that combine to bring about an increasing mobilisation of subjectivity in work.

The limits of this book do not enable me to revisit the debate about capitalism's phases. But a reflection on the fragility of concern for others must carefully weigh the possible consequences resulting from an increased psychological commitment from employees – men and women alike – in work, from the modelling of emotions that seems to condition this commitment and from the apparent use of specific moral resources to perform certain tasks and guarantee certain workplace behaviours.

The Temptation of 'Emotional Capitalism'

Indeed, a vast literature has developed over the past fifteen years that seeks to prove the emergence of a phase of capitalism that it calls emotional, one that no longer demands coldness, but in which generating increased surplus value depends on emotionally mobilising the subjectivity of all workers. According to the argument, far from requiring unfailing indifference, the rearranging of the world of work into disposable fields of competences and existences would rather seem to contrive a situation in which workers develop an intense attention to others.

In the course of their joint work, Michael Hardt and Antonio Negri thus defend the idea, notably when defining their concept of the 'multitude', that an immaterial mode of production characterises our time and makes it very difficult to distinguish commodity production from the social production of various subjectivities, each of which has its own uniqueness. Indeed, instead of removing workers from sociability and directing them towards dead matter, contemporary capitalism sets them within a 'living intersubjectivity',[54] crossed by affects and empirically reflected in the current importance of jobs devoted to human relations of care, upkeep and education. So they argue, immaterial labour, qua 'labor that creates immaterial products, such as knowledge, information, communication, a relationship, or an emotional response',[55] almost always relies on 'emotional work', work that involves arousing or manipulating affects in others such as feelings of comfort, satisfaction, passion. This affective labour, however, produces nothing less than social relationships and forms of life.[56] This is why Hardt and Negri see it as endowed with a potential for positive transformation; immaterial labour, in its very logic, continuously implements new collaborations between ever singular subjectivities, and thus offers the foundations of a constituent power vested in the 'multitude'. Hardt and Negri posit this horizon of emancipation based on their diagnosis that this immaterial labour, whose model proscribes the indifferent and disengaged subject observed by Adorno, has become hegemonic from a qualitative point of view, that is, has now imposed its tendencies on other forms of work, particularly industrial work.

It has also been highlighted that the financialisation of capitalism and the deterioration of working conditions brought on by its forms of management – where the tendency is to demand unlimited subjective competences – blur the boundaries not only between the private and professional public spheres, but also between strategic action and an orientation towards others. Today's 'entreployees', as Honneth and Martin Hartmann point out, are expected not only to dutifully fulfil externally imposed production quotas, but also to bring communicative and emotional skills and resources to bear in order to meet project goals they are more or less responsible for setting.[57]

Light has also been shed on various restricted and standardised uses of empathy. Alexis Cukier, for example, has remarked upon the unequal distribution of the quantity, quality and uses of empathy in social space, which he calls dyspathy. The current organisation of work has rendered certain uses of empathy impossible (e.g. by leading one to have a detached view of the fate of one's colleagues), yet also builds on empathy by directing its still authorised uses, for example by channelling empathy towards certain of the properties of other individuals and groups. Far from being based on the impossibility of attentiveness towards others, contemporary capitalism pulls empathy towards cooperation with one's superiors rather than one's peers and simultaneously enlists it in efforts at peace-building and conflict prevention.[58]

In a more systematic vein, Eva Illouz's work *Cold Intimacies* defines the current form of capitalism as 'emotional capitalism', which she understands as follows:

a culture in which emotional and economic discourses and practices mutually shape each other, thus producing what I view as a broad, sweeping movement in which affect is made an essential aspect of economic behaviour and in which emotional life – especially that of the middle classes – follows the logic of economic relations and exchange.[59]

From the outset, however, Illouz's investigation diverges from Adorno's diagnosis, because for her the world of capitalist labour, far from being devoid of emotions, has always been saturated with affects commanded by an imperative to cooperate.[60] Hers is an attempt is to identify a mutation that began in capitalism some thirty years ago: empathy, under the name of emotional intelligence, has gradually come to be considered a 'professional competence',[61] because it announces an ability to forge and maintain social relationships. Thus companies have introduced it as a criterion by which to evaluate their (prospective) employees. Moreover, the phenomenon spills over into one's close relationships; not only are the emotions that weave the private sphere aligned around this competence, but the market provides the categories in which affectivity in general is conceived and manifested. For this reason, concern for others would appear to be a major cog in the functioning of the world of work, the market and social relations under capitalism.

Counter-Arguments

As more importance is given to this intertwining of the culture of moral dispositions and the blossoming of contemporary capitalism, it seems necessary, first, to stress that only a partial revision of Adorno's thesis is entailed by the fact that capitalism does indeed operate today by instrumentalising and orienting affects – that is, some affects, in certain circumstances and for certain purposes. Christophe Dejours's work indicates this quite clearly by showing how the situation of constant testing and evaluation, forged by new management techniques, has enabled a generalisation of docile participation in 'dirty work' – that is, the manufacture of social injustice, and an insensitivity towards the suffering of others – within the world of work itself.[62] These techniques find an effective complement in the posited equivalence between virility and the ability to inflict violence on others, where indifference becomes an indicator of strength of character and a sense of collective responsibilities. Similarly, the 'moral fitness' of the leader that psychologists have established as an emotional competence, according to Eva Illouz's account, includes not only empathy and a friendly attitude aiming to demonstrate one's ability to cooperate with others but also a capacity for self-control exercised through a *distance* taken from others.[63]

More fundamentally still, the following argument must be made. Performing emotional labour to heighten the intensity of my cooperation and to prove myself capable of inspiring confidence and of understanding the needs of my team members doubtless requires drawing on a type of moral knowledge similar to that underlying the concern of others. Nevertheless, from the moment this concern is defined as both a disposition and a response, as an attention to the needs and suffering of others that is inseparable from the acts that seek to put an end to it, the advent of an emotional era of capitalism – even if the intended affect encourages people to put themselves in the place of others – is not enough to prove, quite to the contrary, the end of generalised indifference within the capitalist form of life.

In addition, contemporary works focus on the mobilisation of moral feelings in workplace relationships, particularly in companies, and on how the know-how it generates infects private relationships. In other words, among the causal elements that Adorno isolates to explain the reign of coldness, the various works cited here deal only with self-preservation. Indeed, through their descriptions of a phase of capitalism characterised by a certain indistinction of instrumental action and attention to others, they highlight a mutation in what Adorno and Horkheimer called the constitutive choice of bourgeois society – to cheat or go under.[64] This choice is constantly performed in a way that henceforth mobilises, in contradiction with Adorno's analysis, affects, and among them forms of empathy. The other dimensions explored by Adorno to shed light on the capitalist form of life, phantasmagoria and fetishism, the withering of experience, commensurability and interchangeability, are not questioned or even addressed by proponents of the thesis of emotional capitalism. Yet, nothing allows us to affirm, and certainly not the current proliferation of immaterial goods, that we are rid of fetishism in the sense of a bewitchment that conceals the traces of human labour which has allowed the commodity to come into existence, and with it the accumulation of capital. Similarly, lived experience, in the sense of the experience arranged by phenomena of remembrance and expectation that make it possible to confront all aspects of a thing or an event, is undoubtedly as much mutilated by the digital texture of our wars as it had been by their technical fury. The pure succession of instantaneous experiences that leave no trace, which has taken the place of *Erfahrung*, was recently documented by Hartmut Rosa in *Acceleration*. His book describes our situation as one in which experiences lack the 'cohesive force for expectations', as an era characterised by a social acceleration such that, individually and collectively, 'the link between the past, the present, and the future is sundered so that supposedly autonomous spaces for organization turn into a static space of fatalistic standstill'.[65] As for the liquidation of the particular that, according to Adorno, is effected within the form of exchange, it is diffracted without end. Generalised commensurability is redoubled and refined by the multitude of phenomena of evaluation that abound within and outside the company, while the fetish of generality within the social sciences and their fascination with their own work of quantification now coincide exactly, leaving nothing over.

On closer examination, the Adornian diagnosis of generalised coldness is therefore not invalidated by the proliferation of works on contemporary capitalism's mobilising of certain moral dispositions; indeed, it is instead clear that a mutation has taken place in one of the motives of indifference to others that Adorno identified – the constant imposing of the logic of self-preservation, which it turns out is apt to feed on forms of attention to others.

Finally, even if there is partial truth in the argument that the borders between concern for others and the imperatives of capitalism are porous, it would in no way invalidate the principle that moral dispositions are unequally distributed along gender lines.

In *Saving the Modern Soul*, Eva Illouz argues that, during the course of the movement of capitalism that she discerned in her previous works, gender distinctions lost their virulence, to such an extent that she speaks of an 'androgenization' of emotional behaviours.[66] The figure of the empathic manager has overcome the masculinised imperative of cold and rational behaviour, which leads Illouz to conclude that the symbolic oppositions between feminine and masculine attributes have withered within the professional world. She even suggests a new emotional stratification: the divide no longer passes between men's and women's emotionality but between the members of working and middle classes, with emotional competence marking membership in an educated and largely globalised group.[67]

And yet it would appear that women are still encouraged to cultivate a surplus of moral feelings, regardless of class belonging, a surplus that always ensures that unpaid work is performed and that also underpins the development of 'ethical' consumerism.

This is unequivocally demonstrated by the aforementioned research into the unchanging distribution of care activities. The emotional element of care is fundamental, first, in so far as its realisation, its success, its adjustment to the concreteness of the situation and the particularity of the needs to be taken care of, depends on a form of concern. Above all, the moral attitude is also a guarantee of someone's disinterestedness in taking care of another person. And this is precisely what contributes to the value of this care – because this is what escapes the quantification of salaried time, or because its compensation itself would appear contrary to its purpose.[68] In this sense, it is concern for others properly speaking that allows for an appropriation of women's work, or indeed for a form of exploitation, if, as Christine Delphy suggests, we stop observing exploitation from the exclusive angle of surplus value, which only covers the particular case of waged labour.[69] Appropriation is not a mere founding event of capitalism; it is a permanent flow, and one of its mechanisms is a moral feeling that, in the main, is attributed to women. Appropriation allows for the accumulation of value (which is not necessarily based on the deduction 'value produced minus paid salary', but is part of a broader logic of usurpation), while ensuring the conditions of possibility of the market, the perpetuation of the social fabric, the reproduction of subjects defined by physical needs.

The gendered surplus of moral dispositions also underpins new markets through the development of 'ethical' consumption, 'fair' trade and 'responsible' purchasing. Numerous studies illustrate the role that women play in the success of this new device in capitalism, which activates a concern for nature whose intrinsic link to the concern for others Adorno and ethicists of care alike postulate.[70] Women are the first buyers and the main targets for the marketing of this form of trade, and in particular of 'cause-related marketing', which is to say campaigns that bring together companies and non-profit associations in the simultaneous promotion of a social or environmental cause and a commodity (for example by paying part of the purchase price of each product sold to an association).[71] Symmetrically, the social sciences have studied the strategies that people who engage in ethical consumption deploy to avoid any threat to their gender identity, strategies that include rationalising this mode of consumption.[72] In this mode, too, capitalism and the gender order reinforce each other mutually through a concern for others.

Viewed in light of recent developments in capitalism and the organisation of care, the argument that moral subjectification is gender-differentiated is thus strengthened. We are given to see the manufacturing of inattentive subjects who constantly 'forget' experiences comprising the suffering and polymorphy of others. In some of these subjects – female subjects – this fundamental coldness becomes sutured to a disposition for care, which itself is confined to forms that are deemed valuable for the market – to its conditions of possibility as well as to its concrete exchanges. The concern for others, by proving to be compatible, in its gendered distribution, with capitalism, forces us to consider a reality that Adorno himself omitted: namely, that generalised commensurability is not the other of incommensurability or singularity, because the latter can indeed nourish the former. In other words, capitalism can be consolidated through incommensurability and singularity, such as emerges with a concern for a particular other, with attentiveness to the uniqueness of his or her needs or suffering, a singularity which is nevertheless dissolved in the process. But this consolidation is based on a confinement of concern to tasks, spheres and a gender, all of which are well defined.

If we look closely, there is not simply an absence of contradiction between a generalised coldness and certain forms of attention to others, an absence of contradiction that has non-gendered manifestations, such as a gendered reality; it seems possible to argue that unaffection is precisely *permitted*, or at least *reinforced* by these limited forms of aliveness towards others. For it must be noted that coldness can no longer be expressed or assumed. The moral subjectification we have described is nowadays enhanced, in both men and women, with a rhetoric of care and feeling. This is illustrated by the waves of 'solidarity' that submerge social networks without ever leaving them, and structure self-exposure on the Internet for purposes of recognition. And this is what is revealed by today's emphasis on putting forward, among other necessary management skills, an ability to put oneself in the place of others, even though the wage relationship is completely shaped by the imperative of self-preservation and forgetting others. Beyond an explanation in terms of the course of history, the appearance of this rhetoric, not yet observable for Adorno, seems to me related to Slavoj Žižek's description of interpellation as a form of subjectivation that succeeds precisely in that the subject concerned perceives itself as being fully a human person. Žižek reminds us that when someone says, 'I am recognized for occupying such and such a place in the social world, but beware, I am not only that, I am much more', that when a subject holds this discourse on itself, we are not dealing with a testimony of interpellation's failure, but on the contrary the surest indication of its ultimate success.[73] It is precisely because I reveal myself and am recognised as attentive to the needs of others that the success of my 'cold' subjectivation is complete.

4 Concern for Others in a Wrong World

Despite his famous assertion that 'there is no right life in a wrong world',[1] Adorno seems to admit that if no one in our administered world leads a morally acceptable existence, there are just (in the sense of apt) gestures – fleeting and tiny ones in the face of the social totality – which eliminate suffering, aim to put an end to intolerable suffering, result from a confrontation with and acceptance of the polymorphy of others, from one's raising one eyes to meet this polymorphy. For example, he repeatedly mentions the acts of the 20 July 1944 conspirators.[2] Far from seeing them as motivated by a will to negotiate the best end they could to the war, to avoid a disastrous surrender and restore Germany's prestige, Adorno illustrates in these passages that moral action is possible even in the most hostile of conditions, and does so to underline the irrational side of the moral act.

Similarly, several passages in his work evoke the fragile motif of love, not the romantic kind – which only seemingly transgresses the logic of exchange and self-preservation and, in its matrimonial concretisations, comes in for robust critique in *Minima Moralia* – but *agapē*. Presuming an ability to be touched by other's destinies, obliging solidarity and help, *agapē* has historically speaking proven rather futile an orientation. This is notably true for Christianity, which sought 'to eradicate the coldness that permeates everything' but ended up neutralising *agapē* by untying it from any project that sought to impact the social order. Love, Adorno tells us, is above all possible only 'for short periods and in very small groups',[3] which he believes utopians like Charles Fourier had been able to see. But what, then, are we to do with these islets, these fulgurations, which, despite the structuring force of the experience of the capitalist form of life, despite the perpetual practice of cold subjectivation, testify, in a fleeting way, to a fragile but embodied concern for others?

How can we grasp these gestures that indeed seek to end suffering or the cruelty of some need – whether we interpret them, like Adorno, as the result of a physical impulse (*Negative Dialectics* enjoins us to live such that we may think we've been 'a good animal'[4]), or whether we see them as indicating a crack in the sort of subjectivity that does not subscribe as readily to the inevitable as others, or whether we explain them, in a more strictly Benjaminian way, as stemming from an involuntary memory that forces us to see the singularity of others, or whether we admit that they can take place within the framework of the gender-based care organised by capitalist society? What remains of them in so far as they occur in a wrong world, in which everyone is necessarily guilty? What effectiveness, what power do they have? What is their value?

There are two different issues we must deal with here. On the one hand, impediments to moral life are not only situated in processes of subjectivation. Because the concern for others exists only in deeds, to understand it we must consider, in addition to the mechanisms that seek to render the disposition itself impracticable, the weight of social formations on the moral gesture and its meaning, the solidity it opposes to them. This is a problem that does not appear as such in care theories but that can be reconstructed from Adorno's philosophy. On the other hand, it seems necessary, in so far as Adorno names reification the – functionally determined – agreement of capitalism and moral dispositions, to answer the question of what it is that remains, of what can remain, of moral content, of rectitude in acts of care that arise from the general economy of affects characteristic of the capitalist form of life.

The Fragility of Caring for Others *in Acts*

Ethicists of care address the question of the possible pointlessness of the moral gesture mainly in the form of a reflection on what constitutes bad care – care that responds to a request that was not made, or was but in different terms. In other words, the failure of the moral act for an ethic of care results mainly from a misinterpretation of another's needs, an inapt adjustment or an insincere concern. As care is primarily thought of as being realised in an intersubjective relationship,[5] a problem arises whenever error, incompetence, clumsiness, or even a desire for power arises on the part of the person giving it. The context itself, it seems, is thus unable to denature the moral gesture.

We must nonetheless consider the possibility that needs or distresses may be actually attended to, but that the responses to them are inadequate, not clumsily but structurally so. This is what Adorno allows us to think when, in *Minima Moralia*, he charges bourgeois virtues such as solicitude with being 'utterly corrupted';[6] or when, in an already quoted passage from *Dialectic of Enlightenment*, he notes with Horkheimer that, in a completely administered society, solidarity with the creature is expressed nowhere more than in an interest in the new Buddhism and the Pekinese.[7] This perversion is in fact each time due to the illusory nature that an historically determined situation can confer on moral actions. Thus, attitudes which, according to Adorno, had something 'good and decent'[8] about them in the form of bourgeois life, and which put into practice virtues such as 'independence, perseverance, forethought, cir-cumspection',[9] have, as attitudes, become inappropriate in a changed social context. The historical and economic conditions on which such virtues of Protestant ethics depended collapsed as Nazism came along and capitalism mutated, although to individuals such was not necessarily apparent.

On occasion Adorno also sheds light on the rudiments of moral life, in so far as they prove out of place in a context full of raw misfortune and pain. The capitalist form of life orders necessities and worth in a way that, in its absurdity, only completes the reign of coldness:

A major crime appears to the individual very largely as a mere infringement of conventions [. . .] The thought of particular indelicacies, however, micro-organisms of wrongdoing, unnoticed perhaps by anyone else – that at a social gathering one sat down too early at table [. . .] – such trifles can fill the delinquent with unconquerable remorse and a passionately bad conscience.[10]

Not only do serious breaches in the concern of others no longer appear to anyone as such, but the few flashes of delicacy and thoughtfulness that remain are belittled and corrupted by the continuous piling up of affronts.

More precisely, Adorno's reflection enables us to delimit the inadequacy that constantly haunts moral gestures, not only because the moral knowledge with which they are realised may prove inadequate, but also and above all because they can be distorted, debased or turned around by the historical context; they are then struck with impotence.

The Impossibility of Moral Knowledge

Late capitalism has produced a context that affects the knowledge that concern for others actualises and requires. This is chiefly why, according to Adorno, there can be no calling for the restoration of morality to simple virtue. His argument against a rational conception of morality adopts some of the criticisms levelled at it by the thinkers of virtue, who depict the moral subject as acting not on the basis of abstract ideas and after a process of discursive reasoning, but in accordance with particular purposes, endeavouring in this way to reconcile the universal and the singular. Adorno nonetheless argues that the concept of virtue now has an 'archaic sound'.[11] The type of moral knowledge it implies and embodies cannot meet the demands that modern societies impose on moral subjects.

Virtue is indeed possible only in a 'circumscribed universe',[12] and is thus made impracticable by the endlessly extending world of today. For Adorno (and this goes beyond his reasoning on virtue), moral knowledge is a knowledge in situation – a knowledge that is negative and reduced to pieces, but a knowledge of the situation.[13] What the situation is, however, is something we can no longer adequately know. Situations, thanks to today's social conditions, are incommensurable with our experiences, or rather, can accordingly no longer be precisely divided up. If the situation can be distinguished from the context, in that it is cut out by the experience had in this situation, then the phenomenon of shock that, according to Benjamin and Adorno, replaces true experience, or *Erfahrung*, precisely dissolves any 'situation'. The event that provokes it only shakes up consciousness; it does not allow itself to be grasped or integrated into a singular story. It engenders an experience that strips one of the means to face up to this event.

Adorno's diagnosis, established in the 1940s and reiterated twenty years later in *Problems of Moral Philosophy*, that having knowledge of the situation is impossible, can be merely reinforced by the current digitalisation of our relationship to the world, which is characterised by continuous exposure to large quantities of information that make both experience and the specific knowledge it bears impossible. The ability to isolate *what is important*, which distinction is at the heart of the concern of others, finds itself engulfed. The ethics of care, as is known, emerged from Carol Gilligan's analysis of the narrative that a little girl, Amy, worked through to solve a dilemma – should Heinz steal the drug that would save his sick wife, since he can't buy it? Where the situation she outlined involved a husband, a wife, medication and a pharmacist, today the flood of digital notifications about other emergencies and other needs, the build-up of information about this woman's chances of survival relative to the advancement of her disease, the constant offers for this same drug – cheaper and produced in China – that appear on the right-hand side of the screen, or even the ubiquity of the social network of both the pharmacist and the husband – all this disturbs a determination of what must be saved and how by drowning what necessarily partial knowledge solicitude gleans from the situation, in data both unlimited and equivalent in ethical weight.

Our universe is also expanding in the sense that more and more hybrid entities, technologies, things, are coming to figure among the elements that make up the moral field, and settling in the fabric of our responsibilities, making more elusive the paths that a concern for others must take. The current densifying of this phenomenon may be illustrated with an example that Michel Callon and Vololona Rabeharisoa provide in an article titled 'La leçon d'humanité de Gino' (Gino's Lesson in Humanity).[14] Gino has a genetic disease called limb-girdle dystrophy. Genetic research has highlighted the existence of healthy carriers of defective genes, something Gino had been unaware of. The research has made him aware of links to ancestors, distant and unknown relatives, but especially to his possible offspring, as well as the obligations that emerge from these links. He becomes carried away by new solidarities, bound to new responsibilities towards his descendants. In other words, scientific research can create new moral obligations through the knowledge it produces, obligations that seem nonetheless to be directly borne by vulnerable bodies and individuals. But Callon's demonstration bears on the fact that, rejecting this scientific knowledge, Gino refuses to consider any new responsibilities – such as one that would consist in hesitating about conceiving a child with a woman carrying the same gene. The situation in which the moral gesture is realised through an attention to the particularity and concreteness of this situation eludes us, and new knowledge produced by technology and science, far from allowing more refined moral knowledge to come into view, only gives rise to confusion.

Just as it immobilises the embodied knowledge that virtue or care implies, the contemporary historical context diverts the effectiveness of moral deliberation. As we have noted, Adorno juxtaposes his plea for the corporeal moment of morality with an emphasis on theory and reflection – without seeking to dissolve this distinction or even to refine the articulation between the two. Far from rejecting reflection on the pretext that it would distort an impulse that is always right, in *Problems of Moral Philosophy* he evokes 'an obligation to follow through the implications of my ideas as far as any individual possibly can'.[15] But knowledge that is morally relevant to the concern for others is still socially conditioned even in this more reflective form. Here the problem is not the infinitely expanding universe as such; it is that this expansion has a meaning, that it is in reality oriented. Understood as an accumulation of data, the production of knowledge likely to feed moral deliberation is socially organised, and there are phenomena of knowledge destruction, which are just as much so. This is demonstrated, for example, by contemporary research into the production of ignorance or 'undone science'[16] – themes left outside the field of scientific or public investigation – which has developed particularly in the field of ecology. That certain premises of knowledge are removed from public space or rendered inoperative because they are declared doubtful by authorities invested with scientific or digital authority directly affects my reflection on what I owe to others or nature. The same is true of the way in which my computer filters and algorithms suggest to me, during my very effort to inform my decision by collecting information, contents close to my preferences and habits, to that which is already obvious or at least acceptable to me. In the end, what is offered to me as objective and exhaustive knowledge is my experience in all its partiality – unfolded, fragmented and recomposed by technology.

Even if there is no concealment of knowledge that might be relevant, the very clash of scales between increasingly incommensurable levels of knowledge makes it difficult to make a timely moral decision. One example of this is 'ethical' consumption, which indeed rests in large part on the provision of data, in particular in terms of measuring my environmental impact (the carbon footprint of a product that is given on the label, for example), but also in terms of a concrete moral effect of my purchases (giving help to a child living in difficult ecological conditions on the other side of the planet). The knowledge thus produced enjoins the recognition of a responsibility that is located at an individual level and obliges one to engage in an act that is certainly not inappropriate from the moral viewpoint. However, the consequence is an erasing of the main causal force that explains the dreaded ecological or human peril, namely the world's commodification and technicisation, not to mention a form of life that is unyielding in its determination to master nature, which it represents as a mere resource. More, the knowledge that produces individual responsibility has a strong gendered effect, since it largely assigns, along with 'fair' purchasing, environmental responsibility to women.

Finally, as Christoph Menke points out in his reading of Adorno, reflection is only likely to generate moral knowledge to the extent that it does not damage but rather strengthens our assurance in our freedom.[17] Yet, within the context of the contemporary capitalist form of life, reflection mainly teaches us that the situation is unable to be grasped or mastered. As Menke puts it, 'Today self-consciousness no longer means anything but reflection on the ego as embarrassment, as realization of impotence: knowing that one is nothing.'[18] The self-reflection that, as aforementioned, is supposed to have replaced moral categories today, is constrained to exhaust itself by drawing on knowledge that, without being erroneous, tends to neutralise moral dispositions by illuminating the improbability of their effectiveness.

None of the possible motivations of concern for others therefore escapes the threat of falsification or neutralisation.

Disadjustments and Reversals

But when Adorno goes beyond the disposition to the moral act itself, his philosophical lesson does not bear so much on moral knowledge, its biases or its difficult constitution. This is perhaps because the objectivity of the suffering that weighs on the human being is such that the knowledge of a situation will not be completely distorted. His main intention is to show that, under the conditions of late capitalism, the capacities for action that continue to be cultivated are *for all practical purposes* vain. The moral gesture and the scene of its actualisation are disadjusted, whereby acts that emerge from the concern for other are neutralised by being distorted.

Tact is the subject of repeated considerations on this theme. In so far as it assumes an accurate ability to affect and shows itself in small gestures, tact requires a delicate attention to the situation and the state of mind of others (it is attuned with 'the specific nature of each human situation'[19]). While it ought not to be confounded with the notion of care, in particular because it is closer to the pole of abstention than of intervention, tact shares many features with care. Adorno himself apprehends tact as a product of the moment in history when the bourgeois freed himself from the constraints of absolutism; tact presupposes a convention, perhaps one under attack, but nonetheless existing. More precisely, it corresponds to a moment when it had seemed possible to reconcile the arbitrary claims of convention with the self-centred expectations of the individual. In the immediate post-war period, however, convention became irrevocably undermined and came to appear entirely devoid of authority, while tact survives only on a standardised list of blind and parodic conventions. When we now remain silent faced with a sensitive issue, we no longer show care and attention towards others but 'empty indifference'.[20] In other words, tact can be used only if it is based on a social convention that it simultaneously respects and subverts. Without this convention, tact misses the singular – its target – which is only possible if it is removed from the substance of a universality. As Antonin Wiser puts it, 'tact affects us only because it is the nuance of an abstract social relationship, which it modulates and bends to the point of overflowing it and reaching the differentiated concrete'.[21] However, the possibility of this bending is linked to a historical configuration that has vanished, crippling the subtle exercise of adjustment that tact permitted.

But this is only one symptom of a phenomenon of general discord. The meaning of the moral act is routinely modified, inverted by the context of late capitalism in which it is carried out. An act can be effective, in the sense that both protagonists perceive it as manifesting a concern for others, and that the response to the perceived need of a singular being effectively relieves this being; however, the effect of this moral act on the social totality can be problematic from a moral point of view. Adorno tells us, for example, that being sociable and affable is like maintaining the illusion that the world of coldness in which we live is one in we may still talk with each other. To talk pleasantly with others, to talk obligingly, only perpetuates silence about what matters. It also means taking part in injustice, in so far as in the egalitarian relationships that seem to emerge in the conversation 'concessions made to the interlocutor debase him once more in the person of speaker',[22] because they by no means impact the relations of domination that pass under this conversation. Adorno develops here the idea that the moral gesture is not defined only by its end and its effect on the limited situation in which it is realised, but encompasses 'the resulting shaping of the world'.[23] A gesture that is not carried out with the intention of changing the form of the world is, in the context of late capitalism, enlisted in its (re)production; it is endowed with a meaning that exceeds that of the scene in which it is undertaken. A contrary but complementary mechanism can be found in the confining to the private sphere of gestures that show a concern for others.[24] The inability of such gestures to take on meaning or trigger an effect beyond the personal context in which they are performed is something that Adorno emphasises as a factor of reversal of the meaning of the moral act. For him, the form of generosity defended by Nietzsche, which, within the capitalist form of life, can at best only be achieved 'on Sunday afternoons, that is, in private life', is completely futile.[25]

The social resignification of certain gestures also runs in the other direction, such that the social context can turn an act that does not arise from any concern for others into a moral gesture, or at least one of decency. Thus it is with the generosity that 'the rich' seem to exercise in private relationships, 'some of which is reflected on those they allow to approach them, all this helps to veil them. They remain the nice, the right people, the better sort, the good. Wealth insulates from overt injustice.'[26] While Adorno here sheds light on how behaviour is perceived as moral because of its generous aspect, though it is the consequence of a completely different logic, and testifies, on the contrary, to a certain detachment from the course of the world, his aim is not to explain this phenomenon by resorting to the motif of misunderstanding, of mistaken identity, or even the ideological veil. This disadjustment is, like the others, structurally produced. There are social positions in which one can refrain from violence, from brutality, from alacrity in indifference and before the inevitable, while benefitting from the fact that others carry them out.

No one escapes, in any case, the objective logic of the social condition that is assigned them by a historical context. Indeed, such logic may be sufficient to disqualify one from the outset as a moral agent, such as being a survivor of genocide: 'just by continuing to live one is taking away that possibility from someone else, to whom life had been denied; that one is stealing that person's life'.[27] Adorno's reasoning does not reduce to some expression of a sense of guilt and is not only the mark of a thought shaped by Auschwitz; it applies equally to other vouchsafed positions, to other dubious privileges. And it becomes directly relevant for the contemporary era, as when Adorno evokes the relentless distribution of utility and uselessness, work and unemployment. According to him, capitalist society determines 'a statistical percentage of people of which it must divest itself in order to continue to live in its bad, existing form'.[28] Even before my possible inadequate knowledge of the situation, what undermines my posture in relation to economic migrants, for example, is the fact that I am not one: the capitalist form of life, the social relations it establishes in its structuring and distribution of work, make me a looter, whether of existence or income. My gesture is thereby always-already rendered inactive.

By inventorying the agents and examples of disadjustment which Adorno points up, often summarily, it is possible to discern the main mechanism of reversal of a moral gesture by the context from which it nonetheless emerges. This mechanism proceeds from the substitution of the particular for the universal or vice versa, from the unification of these two contradictory moments by means of a synthesis that mutilates both, from the pure and simple disappearance of one of the two poles. Regardless of its intention and immediate effect, my gesture loses its moral quality the moment the context of its actualisation blurs the boundaries between these two categories. This is what, as we saw above, happened to tact, whose conditions of possibility were dissolved by the erasure of the universal, induced by the death of the convention. This is what also happens when morality becomes personal, for it dispenses with all objective and public foundations. This may well signify the triumph of strategic reasoning – in this context embracing specific moral principles is like asserting one's own interests – but the problem is also and specifically that the particular is then dressed up as absolute, and thus dissolves itself, because it refutes any universal, to which it must nevertheless oppose itself in order to exist. This is also illustrated by the aforementioned possibility of universalising attention to others, which would represent the elimination of the particular: 'Indiscriminate kindness towards all carries the constant threat of indifference and remoteness to each, attitudes communicated in their turn to the whole.'[29] Even forgetting my particular position, acting as an indeterminate being, not understanding myself as situated and not giving it importance in my deliberations, makes my moral act lose its substance and scope by promoting a false universality that serves the interests of a class and keeps the world as it is.

Adorno's reasoning on the disadjustment caused by the collapse of the categories of the universal and the particular allows us to grasp a type of phenomenon which is exemplified by the possibility of the transformation of an act of care, such as one by which a doctor tries to provide a cancer patient with a few more years of life by trying out a last-ditch and very expensive treatment, an act that, in the current context of a shortage of hospital resources, of rationalisation of medical practices and of evaluation of the performance of health services, is transformed into an intolerable attack on the principles of distributive justice and the equitable distribution of access to care. This leads us to see that the resignification involved is not ideological. Not only is it not the result of machinations woven by powerful people, to use Adorno's formula, but the problem is above all that the historical configuration makes it *true*. A violation of principles of distributive justice and equitable care indeed occurs. The concept of truth at play here must also be clarified: it is a matter of a local truth that is conditioned by a structure that is wrong as a whole.

Moral Powerlessness, Political Power

For Adorno, then, capitalist society structurally prevents the moral acts that, by causing suffering, it nevertheless calls for, from being carried out.

He criticises Kant's moral philosophy, among other things, for not having considered the possibility that a power to act does not exist. Kant's moral philosophy conceives an irresistible injunction to act in accordance with the categorical imperative. But the eventuality that 'circumstances arise in which the ability [to put a good and moral action into practice] is simply absent'[30] is simply ignored. In other words, Adorno blames Kant for dispensing with a reflection on powerlessness. To claim that the moral act is inadequate for structural reasons is indeed to defend an idea of the moral agent's impotence.

The number of times the word 'powerlessness' (*Ohnmacht*) occurs in Adorno's work is fairly high; these occurrences are quite disparate, and though they exceed the scope of his reflections on morality, they are particularly present in *Minima Moralia*. First of all, they deal with a powerlessness against the system, a form of life in which individuals 'cannot rationally determine their lives and the life of the whole'.[31] Quite simply, society has become independent of the individuals who make it up, disarming them before the imperatives of its reproduction. But Adorno does not seek to portray the spectator as a powerless figure up against a world with which she has broken all ties; powerlessness is what appears and condenses in the very attempts to respond to the distress of others. Perfectly cold subjectivities are not impotent; only those are that bear a rift, that feel and accept the impulse of horror at the suffering of others. Adorno's diagnosis of powerlessness is not attempted as though he were a critical theorist observing from a bird's-eye perspective; the powerlessness he evokes is immediately perceptible, one that the individual experiences profoundly.

Powerlessness is also sometimes defined in Adorno's work by an absence of social power, such that it then befalls a specific group. In his 'Reflections on Class Theory' Adorno thus speaks of 'the social impotence of the proletariat',[32] a theme that offers us some clarification on the notion of powerlessness itself. Adorno indeed endeavours to identify in Marx's oeuvre a theory of powerlessness that goes by the name of dehumanisation. According to Adorno, dehumanisation refers to the fact that workers are made strangers to the mechanised work process, which they are no longer able to understand, but also to the fact that workers are brutalised, and *in turn inflict on those who depend on them what has been inflicted on them*. In other words, the concept of powerlessness is directly identified with a form of rendering impossible the concern for others. Adorno notes that Marx associates this phenomenon with a cognitive deficit. But while he follows Marx this far, he then makes two objections: on the one hand, he argues that dehumanisation does not result from propaganda and consists simply in the immanence of the oppressed to the system; on the other, today's work process shapes proletarians even more radically than it did in the past, despite their *understanding it perfectly*.[33] We therefore see here the idea take shape of a powerlessness that is not linked to an inadequate perception of the logics to which individuals are subjected, or the principle of a consciousness that is not, as such, that of power. The phenomenon at issue here is quite distinct, then, from the problem of the impossibility of having adequate moral knowledge. The concept of powerlessness sheds light on a phenomenon, collective or singular, which does not proceed by *incapacitation*, but places the social being, especially when she tries to act on her attention to others and their suffering, in a *situation* of powerlessness.

The disposition to have concern for others and the injunctions it carries collide with a social world that is not only filled with inappropriable objects, but that is able to appropriate the meaning of moral acts and turn them into their opposite, and with forms of social organisation and social relations that the moral agent is not only unable to transform but that have a transformative force on the effects of this agent's moral actions. What causes the distress of others, what is intolerable to me, is simply intangible to me, and the very means of possible action resist me.

The knowledge that I have of my own powerlessness can only deepen the disadjusted aspect of the actions I strive to implement despite everything. The aphorism from *Minima*

Moralia in which Adorno describes the exaggerated scruples of his contemporaries regarding breaches of good manners, such as sitting too early at the table, scruples that go hand in hand with unfailing cynicism regarding a serious crime, does not simply shed light on a context-based reversal of priorities within social morality: it teaches us that these scruples are, in spite of everything, the receptacle of an experience that violently rejects the objectified social order. The individual's indifference to moral failing 'is tinged with the awareness that the incapacity for personal decisions grows'.[34] Slight breaches are then what, despite everything, bring one into contact with the moral element and lead one to feel it 'even in one's skin', for example by blushing. Concern for others lodges in reactions of scorn and retracts into a pure emotion due simply to the subject's awareness of the impotence of their actions.

All the same, Adorno's diagnosis of impotence is not an injunction to give up: in particular, he claims, one cannot on account of one's impotence give up the 'chimerical anticipation of a nobler condition'.[35] Instead, the moral agent's impotence, or the fact that the success of one's moral action depends on conditions over which one has no control, is subject in Adorno to a requirement of politicisation, of transitioning to collective action in order to transform these conditions. The moral act of the individual must be 'extended' to politics.[36] Hegel is acknowledged as having brought the philosophical gaze to bear on the fact that an individual's act is unable to touch a reality that imposes on this individual the very conditions of its act. Adorno concludes that, 'Ever since no unpolitical reflection upon praxis can continue to be valid.'[37]

Adorno ends *Problems of Moral Philosophy* by outlining a theory of resistance. The minimal morality that Adorno's collected reflections sketch converge on a sole prescription: to resist wrong forms of life – to resist the outside world, resist 'everything the world has made of us',[38] resist the form that the administered society gives to our relationships with others. The consequence is that critique is always the correlate of morality. As for political action properly speaking, though Adorno refuses to indicate the direction and form it should take, though he increasingly warns against the illusion of immediacy affecting the political movements of his time and their tendency towards anti-reflective spontaneity, he nevertheless conceives that it is in politics, in collective action, that the possibility of overthrowing the existing situation lies. His work entertains no fascination for any individual practice whose demonstrative power might prove to be transformative, and no glorification of an ethical practice in improvement that would give cause for scandal. For him, it is politics that, albeit devoid of positivity, harbours what remains of a power of acting.

Consequently, 'the quest for the right life is the quest for the right form of politics',[39] while a strong distinction between ethics and politics is a means of extinguishing the possibility of the former by facilitating its delimitation to the private sphere only.

It happens, then, that the other question raised by acting from a concern for others within the capitalist form of life, that is, within a wrong world, the question of the content of truth that it can nevertheless assume, leads us to the same conclusion of the necessary entwinement of morality and politics.

The Question of the Moral 'Wrongness' of Care

Does the taking shape of a general economy of affects within the capitalist form of life mean that we ought to limit the definition of reification to its construal in Adorno, for whom the singular individual's tool-like character implies 'moments of stiffness, coldness, exteriority, brutality'?[40] Or can it, should it, be extended to encompass the process that seizes women, enjoining them to feel emotions and 'express' dispositions that ensure a part of the socially necessary work is performed? But then how does the use of the notion allow us to grasp what an ethic of care might still contain by way of truth-content?

Extending the concept of reification, which covers the twofold movement of a subjection to things – that is, to commodities and their interrelationships – and a transformation of self and one's relationships with others into things, to further encompass the phenomenon of a concern for others *produced* in women, seems defensible on the basis of at least five relatively clear-cut arguments.

(a) The singular subject, in this case the feminine one, takes on the character of a *tool* through capitalism's investment in social relations. Specific forms of state- and market-related arrangements of power determine specific uses of the concern for others in interactions, in order to ensure the reproduction of capitalist society. The sutured subjectification that is the lot of women turns them (much as men but in another way) into a 'function of the gear'.[41] Beyond the intersubjective mechanisms through which it is accomplished, reification is above all a certain instrumental relationship of the whole to the individual.

(b) As argued in the previous chapter, the moral dispositions pertaining to concern for others are cultivated to the extent that they allow and conceal forms of exploitation. Yet, what Lukács intended to show with the concept of commodification in *History and Class Consciousness* is that, pushed along by market exchange and the mechanisation of production, the process of dispossession specific to the exploitation of labour has generalised to all spheres of social life. The intrinsic coupling of exploitation and reification is tied to the fact that, for those who benefit from it, exploitation takes the immediate form of calculations on quantities, while these determinations appear to the worker as qualitative determinations of his entire physical and moral existence: 'Labour-time is not merely the objective form of the commodity he has sold, i.e. his labour-power (for in that form the problem for him, too, is one of the exchange of equivalents, i.e., a quantitative matter). But in addition it is the determining form of his existence as subject.'[42] If, as I have suggested, we abandon the prism of waged labour to conceive of exploitation, and if we conceive the accumulation of value as also resulting from the extortion of labour by the imposition of a moral emotion, it appears that this appropriation also gives a form, an impoverished one, to the lives of certain subjects. There is reification, which is carried out in this case without assuming any form of rigorous quantification, but it precedes precisely by rejecting any explicit commensurability. Lukács had already pointed out that the logic of reification, 'which in the case of Taylorism invaded the psyche, here invades the realm of ethics',[43] and also stressed that, with regard to the probity required of employees, probity is a faculty detached from the entirety of the personality, objectivated in relation to it and that it therefore becomes a thing. The transformation of morality into a resource allows a play on the value produced and constitutes a form of reification.

(c) The idea of subjectification, as outlined in Chapter 3, implies that I attain the quality of subject only to the extent that not only do I allow myself to be inhabited by certain dispositions, but that I cultivate them, refine them, increase their effectiveness and productivity, put them right and combine them. Among the multitude of devices that ensure that concern for others is gendered, the emotional work by which I modify the degree or quality of my feelings to ensure the well-being of others, or the way in which the routine activity of caring to which I am tied conforms my sensitivity and attention to others, unequivocally confirms what Adorno wrote in *Dialectic of Enlightenment*: the bourgeois division of labour requires individuals to mould 'themselves to the technical apparatus body and soul'.[44] The production of a feminine concern for others coincides with a shaping of subjectivity in accordance with, and on the model of, *the productive machine*.

(d) Phenomena concerning the orienting of moral dispositions have a depersonalising, de-singularising dimension, which equally counts among the characteristics of reification. With capitalism's investment in a particular form of concern for others, emotional relations and social relations more broadly are transformed into objects *able to be compared* with one another, and not only in so far as they allow an analysis in terms of costs and benefits. The very idea of rules for feelings implies that moral emotions can be emptied of their particularity, detached from the concrete context in which they are expressed, related to a norm and evaluated according to abstract criteria, all while the serial production of subjects with gender-determined competences deprives caregivers of any singularity.

(e) According to Adorno's own definition, reification is a 'forgetting' of the experiences of others in their suffering and polymorphy, a crude and mechanical forgetting of what is or would have been possible, of the suffering that we inflict, of all the facets that make a person a unique being. From this perspective, too, there is a reification of female subjects because they are subject to an institutionalised and sedimented forgetting in social relations: a forgetting that a woman might not have any concern for others, or not in this way, or not for that other there, a forgetting correlated to all aspects of this subject not situated in the environs of the family and social reproduction, a forgetting of the suffering caused by one's being enframed in these types of activities and by the ensuing dispossession.

It is therefore not simply the symmetrical arrangement of moral dispositions within capitalism – which presumes, on the one hand, that some may enjoy an absence or limitation of concern for others, and, on the other, that others are subject to this same concern – that speaks for an extension of the concept of reification to cover the *production* of these dispositions. The formal affinity between the engendering of concern for others on the one hand and of logics of the machine and exchange on the other, and the function the former fulfils as regards these logics, pleads in itself for a unified use of the idea of reification.

Nevertheless, to speak of reification seems to presume the moral wrongness of the concern for others that such situations produce. On the one hand, the attentiveness to others stemming from such reification serves an order and social relations that are unequivocally 'wrong', in the sense that Adorno speaks of a wrong world. On the other hand, the moral gesture is arrived at in the absence of autonomy, where autonomy is understood as active self-determination in a context rich with possibilities, an autonomy without which, according to a certain conception of common sense, the idea of morality is empty of all content.

Yet, for defenders of this ethics, that care occurs within structures of domination does not imply that it results in the passive determination of women, that it is utterly wrong or false, or that compensation is its only truth – a correction left to be shared by certain pockets of social reality that morality in the sense of a set of principles of justice cannot impact, at least not effectively. That the concern for others has historically flourished under certain conditions of subordination does not imply that its normative content is reduced to that – inexistent – of subordination.

Most of its theorists, Joan Tronto in particular, refuse to conceive of a morality that could and should be separated from social logic and the political field (understood as the field of relations of domination and resistance to it). The complex meaning of the term 'care', at once activity and disposition, both of which have historically been assigned to a particular group, namely women, makes it possible to grasp an object that is moral and yet simultaneously always-already political. From a critical point of view, the strength of the proposal that theories of care put forward lies in the conviction that nothing is gained by ridding care of its historical and social coating, to make it a set of principles as noble as those presented under the title of justice, in order then to reintroduce it into politics.

It seems to me that it is Adorno's moral and political thinking that precisely allows us to conceive of an impure moral object of this type.

First of all, it should be noted that for Adorno all the incarnations of morality, that is, all moral philosophies, but also all forms of moral life, are in any case historical, and bear the mark of a social group. The dianoetic virtues promoted by Aristotle are backdropped by the objective situation of the resigned Hellenistic private citizen, who, out of fear, would refrain from intervening in public affairs.[45] The ideals defended by Nietzsche, such as nobility, are the negative mirror-image of bourgeois morality – these ideals are so thoroughly conceived in opposition to bourgeois norms that they end up being just as situated as the norms they oppose; they are 'feudal values'.[46] And this is even true of Kant's moral philosophy, because the principle of an individual who gives himself his own law, for whom his pure conviction is the law of the world, stands in opposition to any corporatist, feudal or absolutist order. In this respect, it is bourgeois. Therefore, 'even the most abstract distinguishing features of the kind we have encountered in Kant have their place in the real social matrix from which they have arisen'.[47]

Consistent with this, the Adornian idea of resistance, or more precisely his conception of morality as resistance, is not accompanied with any claim to have rid it of all its historical and social dross. Adorno agrees that, even on the few occasions we really are able to refuse society's determinations, we are not really directing our lives, but simply *reacting* to changing forms of oppression. But the impossibility of escaping this determination does not invalidate these negative and minimal prescriptions that require us to resist society and wrong forms of life. With this reminder, Adorno simply removes any presumption of purity or freedom – at least of positive freedom, that is, autonomy – from the conditions of morality.

Even more radically, the new categorical imperative he evokes in *Negative Dialectics*, which commits human beings to determine their thoughts and actions so that Auschwitz is not repeated, is a categorical imperative that is not only 'new', situated in a history, but above all is an imperative that 'has been imposed by Hitler'.[48] Adorno states an unconditional law here, while admitting that the actions of others change the moral texture of the world, and that this imposes obligations on us. Even more fundamentally, he formulates a maxim that is both universal and impartial, even though it arises from a history of brutality and the falsest possible experience of life; it even draws its validity from these latter.

Freedom is not the condition of possibility of the moral gesture. It does not precede this gesture but is realised at the same time as it, what is more, in a limited, reactive form, as resistance, as negation: 'Freedom can be defined in negation only, corresponding to the concrete form of a specific unfreedom.'[49] Therefore, the fact that certain moral gestures are born in and from a general organisation – generated by a reifying totality – of work and affects, is not enough to invalidate them.

It seems to me that the will to conceive of a moral object that is impure is supported, in addition to an insistence on the necessarily historical character of any morality and on a freedom that can only be resistance to unfreedom, by Ador-no's use of the concept of form of life. The *Lebensform* is what permeates the relationships to oneself and the world that precede or rather form the basis of all conceivable ideas of the good life. But forms of life do not only have an ethical texture.

On the one hand, as Rahel Jaeggi has shown, the question posed in *Minima Moralia* 'how should we act?' is not posed directly. It is posed negatively, along with the question: 'What makes us act?'[50] If we cannot establish 'how we must act' without broaching the theme of 'what makes us act', then the fact that dispositions for care and forms of care are inter-twined with the capitalist form of life, that they are made possible by it, does not permit us to dismiss them.

On the other hand, *Minima Moralia* in part seeks to describe the world in which we act, and in which we carry out moral gestures, in its material and institutional arrangement such as this latter influences our actions and our possibilities of life. A form of life is an order of human coexistence that encompasses a bundle of practices and dispositions, as well as their institu-tional but also concrete manifestations and materialisations: it is sedimented in fashion, architecture, legal systems or pat-terns of family organisation. Similar to Benjamin, Adorno con-siders that ideology and forms of thought are joined with the most commonplace objects. These latter bear myth, embody it. But, conversely, they also shape and mediate moral ges-tures. Evoking the way that doors have evolved in bourgeois interiors, Adorno points out that having doors that snap shut of themselves invites the one entering to be inconsiderate.[51] In other words, objects themselves can contribute to forgetting the concern for others, but also neither tact nor solicitude can be grasped without accounting for the door that needs to be closed quietly if they are to be implemented.

What therefore appears to the eye are expectations and moral forms which, inserted in tangible arrangements, but also in relationships of power and domination, do not thereby lose their truth content. The fragility of the concern for others, its dependence on multiple phenomena of suppression and enablement, its intertwining with gender relations, and even its capture by mechanisms that also have effects of reification, do not signify its futility.

Just as, for Adorno, Aristotle's virtues express the political resignation of a given era as much as they open up a horizon of blessed contemplation, the concern for others, as felt and manifested by so many female subjects, ensures the conditions of possibility of the market while offering precarious and undeniable access to the singular and the incommensurable.

Adorno therefore invites us to stop making the moral correctness of an act depend on its origin, or rather on the purity of this origin. For him, true morality rejects any equivalence between the act's moral validity and establishing such through an argument that accompanies or follows the act. But, above all, there can be no relevance in attempting to establish its validity in its (absence of) social matrix. The category of origin is 'a category of dominion. It confirms that a man ranks first because he was there first; it confirms the autochthon against the newcomer, the settler against the migrant.'[52] To this it might be added, in reflection of the gender order: it is a category that reinforces the position of one with a past that is neither shameful nor humble, of one who has never been under anyone's thumb.

In several passages of *Negative Dialectics* where he does not deal with morality, Adorno tells us that the true opposite of reification is dialectics, as a thought of non-identity. The open, or negative, dialectic he envisages is not a method of the golden mean, a way of shedding extremes, as Horkheimer recalled in his 'New York Notes'.[53] If mediation is carried out through extremes, it is not by gradually moving away from them: it is carried out 'in the extremes themselves'.[54] Unlike Hegel, who overcomes oppositions by integrating them into a positive totality, Adorno insists on contradiction, no longer as a 'vehicle of total identification', but as 'the organon of its impossibility'.[55] The dialectic exists only without synthesis; it implies thinking of contradiction as such, posing it as a problem, rather than overcoming it.

On this basis, we must take the full measure of what we stated at the beginning of this book: a moral stance consists in facing the discomfort of a paradox. It does not unfold *despite* the discomfort of a paradox; it unfolds *in a confrontation* with it.

In other words, it implies allowing the conflict between contents and antithetical propositions to remain, 'with rigour and in freedom'.[56] This is posed by the above-cited and key aphorism from *Minima Moralia*, '*Just hear, how bad he was*', in which at issue is the contemporary inversion of small and large difficulties. It points to a dialectic without synthesis, one commanded by the antinomy that haunts Adorno's moral and political reflection, that between the universal and the particular. He reminds us that a moral impulse that directly expresses the universal is frequently a reflection only of absolute alienation, while

he whose moral impulse responds to the wholly external, to fetishized convention, is able, in suffering under the insurmountable divergence between inner and outer, a split that he holds fast in its petrification, to grasp the general without thereby sacrificing himself and the truth of his experience.[57]

Restoring dignity to the particular, making its claims heard, its moral relevance, is possible only if it remains distinct from the universal – as I have pointed out above – but above all only in so far as it remains *in tension* with the universal.

Among the paradoxes with which we must contend, then, is that of spontaneously good motivations, which, though connected with an undeniable concern for others, produce circumstances that are in fact amoral. This is the whole meaning of the theme of the distorting of the moral gesture by the capitalist form of life, of its reversal into its opposite, which we explored in the first part of this chapter. But Adorno also points to the paradox in which a wrong form of life, *because* it is such, nonetheless generates moral effects on the world, such as, for example, concern for others. This is revealed by our reading of concern for others as a practice and disposition that results from a history of domination and yet has some truth content.

In addition, a wrong form of life *produces* critical thought. The self-reflection that now replaces most moral categories, according to Adorno, merges with critique. However, not only does this imply a movement of negation, of determinate negation, but, as Jürgen Habermas argues in *Philosophical and Political Profiles*, Adorno conceives of self-reflection as a faculty whose power comes from the very falsity of its object.[58] The extension of morality to politics to which Adorno summons us is, then, itself the paradoxical result of the falseness or wrongness of the capitalist form of life.

Adorno's sombre meditation on the concern for others should not be understood as acknowledging the end of even the possibility of morality; rather, what Adorno permits us to grasp is that it is against these obstacles that such concern unfolds. He suggests that it is on the basis of its social conditions that we should strive to see it, rather than seek out a mythical origin for it, and then disavow it when this origin is quite clearly nowhere to be found. In other words, doing moral philosophy as a critical theorist implies accepting that one remain in 'the place of carrion, stench and putrefaction'[59]; gender is, without a doubt, one among these places.

A provocative injunction in Adorno, the partiality for putre-faction is a constant premise of feminism, the constraint from which it springs. This is why, by intersecting ethical theories of care with Adornian moral philosophy, by apprehending the concern for others at the same time as capitalism, we have been able to grasp this concern without anchoring it in an anthropological structure, or considering it as existing outside the course of history. It is the partiality for putrefaction that makes morality thinkable not only in its historical, material and social impurity, but precisely *on the basis of* its vulnerability.

Notes

Introduction

1. The overwhelming majority of these theorists are women who defend a resolutely feminist ethics.
2. Tronto, *Moral Boundaries*, p. 127.
3. Adorno, *Negative Dialectics*, pp. 362–3.

Chapter 1

1. Adorno, *Negative Dialectics*, pp. 17–18.
2. Horkheimer, *Dawn and Decline*, p. 13.
3. Marcuse, 'On Hedonism', pp. 119–50.
4. Adorno, *Negative Dialectics*, p. 203.
5. Ibid., p. 285; Adorno, *Metaphysics*, p. 116.
6. Adorno, *Metaphysics*, p. 173.
7. Adorno, *Negative Dialectics*, p. 365.
8. Ibid., p. 365.
9. Menke, 'Tugend und Reflexion', p. 147.
10. Adorno, *Negative Dialectics*, p. 222.
11. Ibid., p. 226.
12. Ibid., p. 229.
13. Adorno, *Problems of Moral Philosophy*, p. 71.
14. Adorno, *Minima Moralia*, p. 182.
15. Paperman, *Care et sentiments*, p. 36.
16. Ibid., p. 32.

17. Noddings, *Caring*, pp. 30–5. Noddings nevertheless refuses to qualify receptivity, which she seeks to define as an 'emotional mode', instead preferring the idea of a 'feeling mode'.
18. Paperman, *Care et sentiments*, p. 26.
19. Kittay, *Love's Labor*, p. 30; Tronto, 'Beyond Gender Differences to a Theory of Care', pp. 644–62; Molinier, *Le Travail du care*, pp. 29–90.
20. Molinier, *Le Travail du care*.
21. Adorno, *Prisms*, p. 235.
22. Adorno and Benjamin, *The Complete Correspondence*, p. 169. This sentence from Adorno is one that Benjamin takes up enthusiastically in one of his letters.
23. Adorno, *Negative Dialectics*, p. 408.
24. Adorno, 'Sociology and Empirical Research', p. 184.
25. Ibid.
26. Adorno, *Minima Moralia*, p. 74.
27. Adorno, *Problems of Moral Philosophy*, pp. 18–19.
28. Adorno, *Hegel: Three Studies*, p. 45.
29. Kittay, 'The Ethics of Philosophizing', p. 122.
30. Brugère, *Le Sexe de la sollicitude*, p. 28.
31. Brugère, 'La sollicitude et ses usages', p. 141.
32. Friedman, 'Beyond Caring', pp. 107–8.
33. Molinier, *Le Travail du care*, pp. 131–3.
34. Adorno, *Problems of Moral Philosophy*, p. 175.
35. Paperman, 'Perspectives féministes sur la justice', p. 421.
36. Garrau, *Care et attention*, p. 47.
37. Molinier, *Le Travail du care*, p. 93.
38. Kittay, 'The Ethics of Philosophizing', p. 122.
39. Molinier, *Le Travail du care*, p. 95.
40. Laugier, 'Frontières du care', pp. 20–2.
41. Adorno, *Negative Dialectics*, p. 365.
42. Adorno, *Problems of Moral Philosophy*, p. 97.
43. Adorno, *Negative Dialectics*, p. 285.
44. Horkheimer and Adorno, *Dialectic of Enlightenment*, p. 93.
45. Adorno, *Problems of Moral Philosophy*, p. 7.
46. Ibid., p. 6.

47. Adorno, *Critical Models*, p. 266.
48. Adorno, *Problems of Moral Philosophy*, pp. 131, 134–5.
49. Ibid., p. 158.
50. Ibid., pp. 164–6.
51. Ibid., p. 166.
52. Horkheimer and Adorno, *Dialectic of Enlightenment*, p. 203.
53. Ibid., p. 207.
54. Adorno, *Problems of Moral Philosophy*, p. 134.
55. Adorno, *Negative Dialectics*, p. 387 (my emphasis).
56. Horkheimer and Adorno, *Dialectic of Enlightenment*, p. 2.
57. Tronto, *Moral Boundaries*, p. 103.
58. Lovell, 'Introduction' to *Face aux désastres*, p. 10.
59. Paperman, 'Les gens vulnérables n'ont rien d'extraordinaire', p. 290.
60. Warren, 'The Power and Promise of Ecological Feminism', pp. 325–45; Raïd, 'De la *land ethic* aux éthiques du care', pp. 173–204.
61. Plumwood, 'Nature, Self and Gender', pp. 3–27.
62. Laugier, 'Frontières du care', p. 8.
63. Adorno, *Critical Models*, pp. 267–8; Adorno, *Metaphysics*, pp. 112–13.
64. Adorno, *Critical Models*, p. 99.
65. I borrow this expression from Fabian Freyenhagen, whose book *Adorno's Practical Philosophy* is subtitled *Living Less Wrongly*.
66. Horkheimer and Adorno, *Dialectic of Enlightenment*, p. 79.
67. Ibid., p. 80.
68. Adorno, *Problems of Moral Philosophy*, pp. 173–4.
69. Capitalism came to be a subject of focus within the constellation of care theories during the 2000s, twenty years after it first emerged, through a reflection on the international organisation of care work, its influence on international migrations, and the 'care drain'. See, for example: Barbara Ehrenreich and Arlie Hochschild (eds), *Global Woman: Nannies, Maids and Sex Workers in the New Economy* (New York: Metropolitan Books, 2003), and Rhacel Parreñas, *Servants of Globalization*: *Women, Migration and Domestic Work* (Stanford: Stanford University Press, 2001). Quite recently, there have been numerous attempts to bend each of these feminist universes towards one another. For example,

see the special issue of *Widersprüche* 'Arbeit am Leben. Care Bewegung und Care-Politiken', and Oksala, 'Affective Labor and Feminist Politics', pp. 281–303.

70. See, for example, Federici, 'Wages against Housework' (1975).
71. Adorno, *Problems of Moral Philosophy*, p. 169.
72. Ibid.
73. Ibid.

Chapter 2

1. Adorno, *Critical Models*, p. 202.
2. Ibid., p. 195.
3. See, for example, Adorno, *Minima Moralia*, p. 49.
4. Benjamin, 'On Some Motifs in Baudelaire', pp. 152–9.
5. Benjamin, 'Experience and Poverty', p. 734.
6. Horkheimer and Adorno, *Dialectic of Enlightenment*, p. 179.
7. Adorno, *Quasi una fantasia*, p. 5.
8. Horkheimer and Adorno, *Dialectic of Enlightenment*, p. 135.
9. Adorno, *Minima Moralia*, p. 54.
10. See Section 'Gaps', Chapter 1.
11. Adorno, *Negative Dialectives*, p. 39.
12. Adorno, *Critical Models*, p. 199.
13. Horkheimer and Adorno, *Dialectic of Enlightenment*, p. 4.
14. Adorno, 'Sociology and Empirical Research', p. 184.
15. Adorno, *Negative Dialectics*, p. 146 (translation modified).
16. Adorno, *Prisms*, pp. 207–8 (my emphasis).
17. Adorno, *Minima Moralia*, p. 63.
18. Horkheimer and Adorno, in Horkheimer, *Gesammelte Schriften Band 12*, p. 470.
19. The idea is that to be able to exchange two commodities, it is necessary to compare them with a third. For this abstraction must be made of the concrete qualities of the commodities involved in this relation. For Marx, this third element is labour, considered as the simple 'time' necessary to produce the commodity in question. For Sohn-Rethel, the abstraction made is that of usage; it is produced by value.

20. Adorno, *Negative Dialectics*, p. 146.
21. Adorno, *Minima Moralia*, p. 229.
22. Jappe, 'Préface' to Sohn-Rethel, *La Pensée-marchandise*, p. 12.
23. Sohn-Rethel, *La Pensée-marchandise*, p. 44.
24. Adorno, *Introduction to Sociology*, p. 31.
25. Sohn-Rehel, *La Pensée-marchandise*, p. 103.
26. Adorno, *Negative Dialectics*, p. 362.
27. Horkheimer and Adorno, *Dialectic of Enlightenment*, p. 65.
28. Adorno, *Minima Moralia*, p. 77.
29. Adorno, *Critical Models*, p. 248.
30. Ibid., p. 270.
31. Adorno, 'Ideology', p. 185.
32. Ibid., p. 189.
33. Adorno, *Negative Dialectics*, p. 148.
34. Horkheimer and Adorno, *Dialectic of Enlightenment*, p. 122.
35. See Adorno, *In Search of Wagner*, in particular Chapter 6, 'Fantasmagoria', pp. 74–85.
36. For a detailed analysis of Adorno's borrowings and rejections of Benjaminian notions, see Moutot, *Essai sur Adorno*, pp. 43–139.
37. Adorno, *Critical Models*, pp. 200–1.
38. Adorno, 'Letter from 10 November 1938', *Theodor W. Adorno and Walter Benjamin: The Complete Correspondence, 1928–1940*, pp. 281–2.
39. Adorno, 'On the Fetish-Character in Music and the Regression in Listening'.
40. Adorno, *Critical Models*, p. 274.
41. Adorno, 'Sociology and Psychology', p. 80.
42. Horkheimer and Adorno, *Dialectic of Enlightenment*, p. 49.
43. Ibid.
44. Bernstein, *Disenchantment and Ethics*, p. 400.
45. Adorno, *Minima Moralia*, p. 41.
46. Horkheimer and Adorno, *Dialectic of Enlightenment*, p. 67.
47. Adorno, *Negative Dialectics*, p. 312.
48. Horkheimer and Adorno, *Dialectic of Enlightenment*, p. 191.
49. Ibid. (my emphasis). Translation modified – SC.
50. Adorno, *Minima Moralia*, p. 68.

51. Honneth, 'A Physiognomy of the Capitalist Form of Life', p. 50.
52. Honneth, *Reification*, p. 38.
53. Ibid., pp. 57–8 (my emphasis).
54. Ibid., p. 56.
55. And in his work 'moral' cannot be understood as signalling towards a perfectionist ethics, as referring to a responsibility that we have towards ourselves.
56. See Seel, 'Anerkennende Erkenntnis. Eine normative Theorie des Gebrauchs von Begriffen', pp. 42–63.
57. Honneth, *Reification*, p. 57.
58. Adorno, *Minima Moralia*, p. 63.
59. Adorno, Letter dated '29 February 1940', *Theodor W. Adorno and Walter Benjamin: The Complete Correspondence, 1928–1940*, p. 321.
60. Ibid., p. 405.
61. Adorno, *Prisms*, p. 223.
62. Adorno, *Introduction to Sociology*, p. 150.
63. Honneth, *Reification*, p. 62.
64. Adorno, *Minima Moralia*, p. 122.
65. See, for example, Adorno, *Problems of Moral Philosophy*.
66. Honneth, *Reification*, p. 57.
67. Honneth, 'A Physiognomy of the Capitalist Form of Life', pp. 186–7.
68. Adorno, *Minima Moralia*, p. 229.
69. Adorno, *Negative Dialectics*, p. 278.
70. Ibid., p. 191.
71. Adorno, 'Individuum und Organisation', p. 441.
72. Adorno, Letter dated '22 September 1937', Adorno and Benjamin, *The Complete Correspondence, 1928–1940*, p. 212.
73. Bernstein, *Disenchantment and Ethics*, pp. 189ff.
74. Adorno, 'Theses on Need', p. 102.
75. Adorno, *Negative Dialectics*, pp. 221–2.
76. Adorno, 'The Idea of Natural History', p. 117.
77. On this paradox, see Cook, *Adorno on Nature*, p. 55.
78. Adorno, 'Theses on Need', p. 102.
79. Adorno, *Negative Dialectics*, pp. 354–5. (Translation modified – SC.)
80. Adorno, *Minima Moralia*, p. 152. (Translation modified – SC.)

81. Adorno, *The Jargon of Authenticity*, pp. 113–15.

82. Adorno, *Minima Moralia*, p. 154.

83. Ibid., p. 153.

84. Adorno, 'Individuum und Organisation', p. 450.

85. Adorno, 'Notizen zur neuen Anthropologie'.

86. Horkheimer and Adorno, *Dialectic of Enlightenment*, p. 159.

87. Ibid., p. 166.

88. Adorno, 'Individu et société', p. 170.

89. Jessica Benjamin, 'The End of Internalization', p. 59.

90. Horkheimer and Adorno, in Horkheimer: *Gesammelte Schriften, Band 12*, p. 523.

Chapter 3

1. Adorno, *Critical Models*, p. 198.

2. Fraser, 'Behind Marx's Hidden Abode', pp. 61–3.

3. Chizuko, 'From Labor of Love to Care Work'.

4. Horkheimer and Adorno, *Dialectic of Enlightenment*, p. 208.

5. Adorno, *Minima Moralia*, p. 60.

6. Adorno to Erich Fromm, 16 November 1937, in Adorno, *Briefe und Briefwechseln IV, 1, 1927–1937*, p. 543.

7. Horkheimer and Adorno, *Dialectic of Enlightenment*, p. 166.

8. Adorno, *Minima Moralia*, p. 96.

9. Jessica Benjamin, 'Authority and Family Revisited or a World without Fathers', in particular pp. 51–7. She herself borrows the expression from Alexander Mitscherlich. See also Jessica Benjamin, 'The End of Internalization'.

10. Adorno, *Minima Moralia*, p. 23.

11. Ibid., p. 92.

12. Ibid., p. 95.

13. Horkheimer and Adorno, *Dialectic of Enlightenment*, p. 206.

14. Ibid., p. 86.

15. Ibid., p. 84.

16. Ibid., p. 206 (my emphasis).

17. Adorno to Erich Fromm, 16 November 1937, in Adorno, *Briefe und Briefwechseln IV, 1, 1927–1937*, pp. 539–45.

18. Ibid., p. 545.

19. Ibid., p. 542 (my emphasis).

20. Adorno, *Prisms*, p. 81 (translation modified).

21. Ibid.

22. Adorno to Erich Fromm, 16 November 1937, in Adorno, *Briefe und Briefwechseln IV, 1, 1927–1937*, p. 543.

23. Horkheimer and Adorno, *Dialectic of Enlightenment*, p. 58.

24. See, for example, Van Nistelrooij, 'Self-sacrifice and Self-affirmation within Care-giving'.

25. Adorno, *Minima Moralia*, p. 91.

26. Ibid., p. 93.

27. Horkheimer, 'Authoritarianism and the Family Today', p. 366.

28. In the major study on *The Authoritarian Personality*, published in 1950, Adorno barely even addresses the question of gender in the chapters that he wrote. Instead, it was a psychoanalyst, Else Frenkel-Brunswik, who would highlight a correlation between the stereotyped images of masculinity and of femininity and the rigidity and conformism that constitute a potential breeding-ground for fascism. According to Frenkel-Brunswik, pre-fascist masculinity is characterised by boastfulness about such traits as energy, independence and will power, and finding passivity intolerable. Women presenting an authoritarian character manifest a pseudo-femininity: while believing themselves to be soft and feminine they manifest a crude aggression, especially towards men. Adorno et al., *The Authoritarian Personality*, chapters X, XI and XII, especially pp. 428ff.

29. Adorno, *Études sur la personnalité autoritaire*, p. 298.

30. Horkheimer and Adorno, *Dialectic of Enlightenment*, p. 208.

31. Adorno, *Critical Models*, p. 94.

32. Irigaray, 'Mères et filles vues par Luce Irigaray. Entretien'.

33. Horkheimer and Adorno, *Dialectic of Enlightenment*, p. 207.

34. Ibid., p. 208.

35. Some among them have adopted an essentialist approach to this division. There can be no question of examining their works here.

36. Tronto, *Moral Boundaries*, p. 103.

37. Gilligan, *In a Different Voice*, p. 70.

38. Molinier, Laugier and Paperman, 'Introduction', in *Qu'est-ce que le care?*, p. 14.

39. Deutscher, 'Judith Butler, Precarious Life, and Reproduction'.

40. Laugier, 'Le sujet du care', in *Qu'est-ce que le care?*, p. 187.

41. Hochschild, *The Managed Heart*, p. 56.

42. Ibid., p. 110.

43. Paperman and Molinier (eds), *Contre l'indifférence des privilégiés. À quoi sert le care?*

44. See Nel Noddings's book *Caring*.

45. Bubeck, *Care, Justice and Gender*.

46. To take up the definition of exploitation given by Christine Delphy in *Pour une théorie générale de l'exploitation*.

47. We also find the very classic thesis of differentiated socialisation. Thus Carol Gilligan recently defended the idea of the deployment by the patriarchal regime of a masculine socialisation that emits an impossibility to think in relation, and therefore to experience the responsibility that relationships attract. With this, empathy and the ability to cooperate atrophy (Gilligan, 'Résister à l'injustice: une éthique féministe du care').

48. Tronto, *Moral Boundaries*, p. 121.

49. Tronto, 'Beyond Gender Differences to a Theory of Care', p. 654.

50. Damamme and Paperman, 'Care domestique: délimitations et transformations'.

51. See, for example, Pailhe and Solaz, *Entre famille et travail, des arrangements de couples aux pratiques des employeurs*; Méda, 'Pourquoi et comment mettre en œuvre un modèle à deux apporteurs de revenus/deux pourvoyeurs de soins?'

52. Molinier, *Le Travail du care*, p. 172.

53. Ibos, 'Du macrocosme au microcosme, du vaste monde à l'appartement parisien, la vie morale de la Nounou', p. 127.

54. The expression is Stéphane Haber's from 'La puissance du commun', *La Vie des idées*, 31 March 2010. URL: http://www.lavie-desidees.fr/La-puissance-du-commun.html

55. Hardt and Negri, *Multitude: War and Democracy in the Age of Empire*, p. 108.

56. Ibid., p. 110.

57. Hartmann and Honneth, 'Paradoxes of Capitalism', p. 49.
58. Cukier, 'Pouvoir et empathie', in particular pp. 375–411.
59. Illouz, *Cold Intimacies*, p. 5.
60. Illouz, *Saving the Modern Soul*, p. 81.
61. Illouz, *Cold Intimacies*, p. 90.
62. Dejours, *Souffrance en France*.
63. Illouz, *Saving the Modern Soul*, p. 82.
64. Horkheimer and Adorno, *Dialectic of Enlightenment*, p. 75.
65. Rosa, *Social Acceleration*, p. 296.
66. Illouz, *Saving the Modern Soul*, p. 15.
67. Ibid., p. 150.
68. Ueno Chizuko thus highlights the active opposition of Japanese women to the renumeration of their care labour based on their conviction that the work at stake is invaluable, done out of love. Chizuko, 'From Labor of Love to Care Work'.
69. 'We must stop defining exploitation as a monetary balance.' Delphy, *Pour une théorie générale de l'exploitation*, p. 104.
70. See, for example, 'Comment consomment les hommes et les femmes', *Report from CREDOC* no. 209, December 2013.
71. Hawkins, 'Shopping to Save Lives: Gender and Environment Theories Meet Ethical Consumption'.
72. Shang and Peloza, 'Can Real Men Consume Ethically?'
73. Žižek, *The Ticklish Subject*, p. 258.

Chapter 4

1. Adorno, *Minima Moralia*, p. 36.
2. See, for example, the first lecture of his *Problems of Moral Philosophy*.
3. Adorno, *Critical Models*, p. 202.
4. Adorno, *Negative Dialectics*, p. 299.
5. Some theorists call to dissociate care and this dyad, but often the exercise is only successful when it comes to thinking about the political significance of care and the issues of justice inherent in its social distribution. The activity of caring itself is generally described within the context of an intersubjective relationship.
6. Adorno, *Minima Moralia*, p. 34.

7. Horkheimer and Adorno, *Dialectic of Enlightenment*, p. 208.

8. Adorno, *Minima Moralia*, p. 34.

9. Ibid.

10. Ibid., p. 180.

11. Adorno, *Problems of Moral Philosophy*, p. 98.

12. Ibid.

13. See section 'What Counts as Moral Reasoning' in Chapter 1 above.

14. Callon and Rabeharisoa, 'La leçon d'humanité de Gino'.

15. Adorno, *Problems of Moral Philosophy*, p. 163.

16. Frickel et al., 'Undone Science: Charting Social Movement and Civil Society Challenges to Research Agenda Settings'.

17. Menke, 'Tugend und Reflexion', pp. 154–5.

18. Adorno, *Minima Moralia*, p. 50.

19. Ibid., p. 36.

20. Ibid., p. 37.

21. Wiser, 'Le tact, expérience de la littérature ou Proust lu par Adorno'.

22. Adorno, *Minima Moralia*, p. 26.

23. Adorno, *Problems of Moral Philosophy*, p. 162.

24. We also come across this theme in care ethics, especially in the work of Joan Tronto, who conceives the opposition between public life and private life as one of the boundaries of morality that contributes to devalorising care. See *Moral Boundaries*, pp. 10ff.

25. Adorno, *Problems of Moral Philosophy*, p. 173.

26. Adorno, *Minima Moralia*, p. 186.

27. Adorno, *Metaphysics*, p. 113.

28. Ibid.

29. Adorno, *Minima Moralia*, p. 77.

30. Adorno, *Problems of Moral Philosophy*, p. 75 (my emphasis).

31. Adorno, *Negative Dialectics*, p. 112.

32. Adorno, 'Reflections on Class Theory', p. 107.

33. The division of labour means that 'individual work processes are increasingly undifferentiated, so that the man who can perform one can perform virtually all and can understand the whole operation ('Reflections on Class Theory', p. 108).

34. Adorno, *Minima Moralia*, pp. 180–1.
35. Ibid., p. 44.
36. The expression is Christoph Menke's from 'Tugend und Reflexion', p. 160.
37. Adorno, *Critical Models*, p. 264
38. Adorno, *Problems of Moral Philosophy*, p. 168.
39. Ibid., p. 176.
40. Adorno, 'Individu et organisation', p. 161.
41. Ibid., p. 167.
42. Lukács, *History and Class Consciousness*, p. 167.
43. Ibid., p. 99.
44. Horkheimer and Adorno, *Dialectic of Enlightenment*, p. 23.
45. Adorno, *Critical Models*, p. 267.
46. Adorno, *Problems of Moral Philosophy*, p. 173.
47. Ibid., p. 152.
48. Adorno, *Negative Dialectics*, p. 365.
49. Ibid., p. 231.
50. Jaeggi, 'Kein Einzelner vermag etwas dagegen', pp. 117ff.
51. Adorno, *Minima Moralia*, p. 40.
52. Adorno, *Negative Dialectics*, p. 155.
53. Horkheimer, 'New Yorker Notizen', in *Gesammelte Schriften Band 12*, p. 297.
54. Adorno, *Hegel: Three Studies*, p. 9.
55. Adorno, *Negative Dialectics*, p. 153.
56. Adorno, *Minima Moralia*, p. 181.
57. Ibid. (my emphasis).
58. Habermas, *Philosophical-Political Profiles*, p. 106.
59. To adopt the expression that Adorno uses in *Metaphysics*, to designate those spaces that metaphysics scorns, though 'these are exactly the things which matter / alors que c'est bien là que les choses se passent' (p. 117).

Bibliography

'Arbeit am Leben. Care Bewegung und Care-Politiken', special issue of *Widersprüche*, 34 (2014).

'Comment consomment les hommes et les femmes', *Rapport du CREDOC*, 209 (December 2013).

Adorno, Theodor W., Frenkel-Brunswik, Else, Levinson, Daniel J. and Sandford, R. Nevitt, *The Authoritarian Personality*, Studies in Prejudice Series (New York: Harper & Brothers, 1950).

Adorno, Theodor W., *Briefe und Briefwechseln IV, 1, 1927–1937* (Frankfurt: Suhrkamp, 2003).

Adorno, Theodor W., *Critical Models: Interventions and Catchwords*, trans. Henry W. Pickford (New York: Colombia University Press, 2005).

Adorno, Theodor W., *Études sur la personnalité autoritaire* (Paris: Allia, 2007).

Adorno, Theodor W., *Hegel: Three Studies*, trans. Shierry Weber Nicholsen (Cambridge, MA: MIT Press, 1993).

Adorno, Theodor W., 'The Idea of Natural History', *Telos*, 60 (1984), pp. 111–24.

Adorno, Theodor W., 'Ideology', *Aspects of Sociology* (Boston, MA: Beacon Press, 1972).

Adorno, Theodor W., *In Search of Wagner*, trans. Rodney Livingstone (London: Verso, 2005).

Adorno, Theodor W., 'Individu et société', in *Société: intégration, désintégration*, trans. Pierre Arnoux, Julia Christ, Georges Felten and Florian Nicodème (Paris: Payot, 2011), pp. 159–79.

Adorno, Theodor W., 'Individuum und Organisation', in *Gesammelte Schriften VIII*, ed. Rolf Tiedemann, in cooperation with Gretel Adorno, Susan Buck-Morss and Klaus Schultz (Frankfurt: Suhrkamp).

Adorno, Theodor W., *Introduction to Sociology* (Cambridge: Polity Press, 2000).

Adorno, Theodor W., *The Jargon of Authenticity*, trans. Knut Tarnowski and Frederic Will (Evanston: Northwestern University Press, 1973).

Adorno, Theodor W., *Metaphysics: Concept and Problems* (Cambridge: Polity Press, 2000).

Adorno, Theodor W., *Minima Moralia*, trans. E. F. N. Jephcott (London: Verso, 2005).

Adorno, Theodor W., *Negative Dialectics*, trans. E. B. Ashton (London and New York: Routledge, 1990).

Adorno, Theodor W., 'Notizen zur neuen Anthropologie', in *Adorno Horkheimer Briefwechsel 1927–1969*, vol. II: 1938–1944 (Frankfurt: Suhrkamp, 2004), pp. 453–72.

Adorno, Theodor W., 'On the Fetish-Character in Music and the Regression in Listening', in *Adorno. Essays on Music*, trans. Susan H. Gillespie (Oakland: University of California Press, 2002), pp. 270–99.

Adorno, Theodor W., *Prisms*, trans. Samuel and Shierry Weber (Cambridge, MA: MIT Press, 1981).

Adorno, Theodor W., *Problems of Moral Philosophy. Nachgelassene Schriften IV*, vol. 10 (Frankfurt: Suhrkamp, 1997).

Adorno, Theodor W., *Quasi una fantasia: Essays on Modern Music*, trans. Rodney Livingstone (London: Verso, 1998).

Adorno, Theodor W., 'Reflections on Class Theory', in *Can One Live after Auschwitz? A Philosophical Reader*, ed. Rolf Tiedmann, trans. Rodney Livingston (Stanford: Stanford University Press, 2003).

Adorno, Theodor W., 'Sociology and Empirical Research', *The Adorno Reader*, ed. Brian O'Conner (Oxford and Malden, MA: Blackwell), pp. 174–92.

Adorno, Theodor W., 'Sociology and Psychology' (part 1), *New Left Review*, 46 (November–December 1967), pp. 67–80.

Adorno, Theodor W., 'Theodor W. Adorno's "Theses on Need"', trans. Martin Shuster and Iain Macdonald, *Adorno Studies*, 1:1 (January 2017).

Adorno, Theodor W., *Vorlesung zur Einleitung in die Soziologie* (Frankfurt: Suhrkamp, 1993).

Adorno, Theodor W. and Benjamin, Walter, *The Complete Correspondence, 1928–1940*, ed. Henri Lonitz, trans. Nicholas Walker (Cambridge: Polity, 1999).

Adorno, Theodor W., Frenkel-Brunswik, Else, Levinson, Daniel J. and Sanford Nevitt, *The Authoritarian Personality: Studies in Prejudice Series* (New York: Harper & Brothers, 1950).

Benjamin, Jessica, 'Authority and Family Revisited or a World without Fathers', *New German Critique*, 13 (1978), pp. 35–57.

Benjamin, Jessica, 'The End of Internalization. Adorno's Social Psychology', *Telos*, 32 (1977), pp. 42–64.

Benjamin, Walter, 'Experience and Poverty', in Michael W. Jennings, Howard Eiland and Gary Smith (eds), *Walter Benjamin: Selected Writings*, vol. 2, part 2, 1931–34 (Cambridge, MA: Belknap Press, 1999).

Benjamin, Walter, 'On Some Motifs in Baudelaire', *Illuminations*, ed. Hannah Arendt, trans. Harry Zohn (London: FontanaPress, 1992), pp. 152–96.

Bernstein, Jay M., *Disenchantment and Ethics* (Cambridge: Cambridge University Press, 2001).

Brugère, Fabienne, *Le Sexe de la sollicitude* (Lormont: Le Bord de l'Eau, 2014).

Brugère, Fabienne, 'La sollicitude et ses usages', *Cités*, 4 (2009), pp. 139–58.

Bubeck, Dietmut, *Care, Justice and Gender* (Oxford: Clarendon Press, 1995).

Callon, Michel and Rabeharisoa, Vololona, 'La leçon d'humanité de Gino', *Réseaux*, 95 (1999), pp. 197–233.

Chizuko, Ueno, 'From Labor of Love to Care Work', oral presentation, 'The Meaning of Care in Different Traditions', Workshop, Doshisha University, Kyoto, 14 March 2016.

Cook, Deborah, *Adorno on Nature* (Durham: Acumen, 2011).

Cukier, Alexis, 'Pouvoir et empathie: philosophie sociale, psychologie et théorie politique', PhD thesis, Université de Paris-Ouest Nanterre, 2014.

Damamme, Aurélie and Paperman, Patricia, 'Care domestique: délimitations et transformations', in Pascale Molinier, Sandra Laugier and Patricia Paperman (eds), *Qu'est-ce que le care?*, pp. 133–57.

Dejours, Christophe, *Souffrance en France. La banalisation de l'injustice sociale* (Paris: Seuil, 1998).

Delphy, Christine, *Pour une théorie générale de l'exploitation. L'extorsion du travail non-libre* (Paris: Éditions Syllepse, 2015).

Deutscher, Penelope, 'Judith Butler, Precarious Life, and Reproduction: From Social Ontology to Ontological Tact', in *Foucault's Futures: A Critique of Reproductive Reason* (New York: Columbia University Press, 2017).

Ehrenreich, Barbara and Hochschild, Arlie (eds), *Global Woman: Nannies, Maids and Sex Workers in the New Economy* (New York: Metropolitan Books, 2003).

Federici, Silvia, 'Wages against Housework', *Revolution at Point Zero: Housework, Reproduction and Feminist Struggle* (New York: PM Press/Common Notions, 2012).

Fraser, Nancy, 'Behind Marx's Hidden Abode: For an Expanded Conception of Capitalism', *New Left Review*, 86 (March–April 2014), pp. 55–72.

Freyenhagen, Fabian, *Adorno's Practical Philosophy: Living Less Wrongly* (Cambridge: Cambridge University Press, 2013).

Frickel, Scott, Gibbon, Sahra, Howard, Jeff, Kempner, Joanna, Ottinger, Gwen and Hess, David J., 'Undone Science: Charting Social Movement and Civil Society Challenges to Research Agenda Settings', *Science, Technology, Human Values*, 35:4 (2010), pp. 444–73.

Friedman, Marilyn, 'Beyond Caring: The De-Moralization of Gender', *Canadian Journal of Philosophy*, 13 (1987), pp. 87–110.

Garrau, Marie, *Care et attention* (Paris: Presses universitaires de France, 2014).

Gilligan, Carol, 'Résister à l'injustice: une éthique féministe du care', in Patricia Paperman and Pascale Molinier (eds), *Contre l'indifférence des privilégiés. À quoi sert le care?* (Paris: Payot, 2013), pp. 35–67.

Gilligan, Carol, *Une voix différente: pour une éthique du care* (Paris: Flammarion, 2008).

Habermas, Jürgen, *Philosophical-Political Profiles* (Cambridge, MA: The MIT Press, 1983).

Hardt, Michael and Negri, Antonio, *Multitude: War and Democracy in the Age of Empire* (London: Penguin, 2004).

Hartmann, Martin and Axel, Honneth, 'Paradoxes of Capitalism', *Constellations*, 13:1. (March 2006), pp. 41–58.

Hawkins, Roberta, 'Shopping to Save Lives: Gender and Environment Theories Meet Ethical Consumption', *Geoforum*, 43:4 (2012), pp. 750–9.

Hochschild, Arlie, *The Managed Heart: Commercialization of Human Feeling* (Berkeley: University of California Press, 1983).

Honneth, Axel, 'A Physiognomy of the Capitalist Form of Life: A Sketch of Adorno's. Social Theory', *Constellations* 21:1 (2005), pp. 50–64.

Honneth, Axel, *Reification: A New Look at an Old Idea*, ed. and intro. Martin Jay (London: Oxford University Press, 2008).

Honneth, Axel, *La Société du mépris: vers une nouvelle théorie critique* (Paris: La Découverte, 2006).

Horkheimer, Max, 'Authoritarianism and the Family Today', in Ruth Anshen (ed.), *The Family: Its Function and Destiny* (New York: Harper and Brothers, 1949), pp. 359–74.

Horkheimer, Max, *Dawn and Decline* (New York: Seabury Press, 1978).

Horkheimer, Max, *Gesammelte Schriften Band 12: Nachgelassene Schriften 1931–1949* (Frankfurt: Fischer Verlag, 1985).

Horkheimer, Max and Adorno, Theodor W., *Dialectic of Enlightenment*, trans. Edmund Jephcott (Stanford: Stanford University Press, 2002).

Horkheimer, Max and Adorno, Theodor W., *Le Laboratoire de la Dialectique de la raison* (Paris: Éditions de la MSH, 2013).

Ibos, Caroline, 'Du macrocosme au microcosme, du vaste monde à l'appartement parisien, la vie morale de la Nounou', *Multitudes*, 37–8 (2009), pp. 123–31.

Illouz, Eva, *Cold Intimacies: The Making of Emotional Capitalism* (Cambridge: Polity, 2007).

Illouz, Eva, *Saving the Modern Soul: Therapy, Emotions, and the Culture of Self-Help* (Berkeley: University of California Press, 2008).

Irigaray, Luce, 'Mères et filles vues par Luce Irigaray. Entretien', *Libération*, 21 May 1979.

Jaeggi, Rahel, 'Kein Einzelner vermag etwas dagegen: Adornos Minima Moralia als Kritik von Lebensformen', in Axel Honneth (ed.), *Dialektik der Freiheit, Frankfurter Adorno Konferenz 2003* (Frankfurt: Suhrkamp, 2005), pp. 115–41.

Jappe, Anselm, 'Préface' to Alfred Sohn-Rethel, *La Pensée-marchandise* (Bellecombe-en-Bauge: Éditions du Croquant, 2010), pp. 7–38.

Kittay, Eva Feder, 'The Ethics of Philosophizing: Ideal Theory and the Exclusion of People with Severe Cognitive Disabilities', in Lisa Tessman (ed.), *Feminist Ethics and Social and Political Philosophy: Theorizing the Non-Ideal* (Berlin and Heidelberg: Springer, 2009), pp. 121–46.

Kittay, Eva Feder, *Love's Labor: Essays on Women, Equality and Dependency* (New York: Routledge, 1999).

Kittay, Eva Feder, 'Une éthique de la pratique philosophique', in Sandra Laugier (ed), *Tous vulnérables? Le care, les animaux et l'environnement* (Paris: Payot, 2012).

Laugier, Sandra, 'Frontières du care', in Sandra Laugier (ed.), *Tous vulnérables? Le care, les animaux, l'environnement* (Petite Bibliothèque Payot, 2012).

Laugier, Sandra, 'Le sujet du care', in Pascale Molinier, Sandra Laugier and Patricia Paperman (eds), *Qu'est-ce que le care?* (Paris: Payot, 2010), pp. 159–201.

Lovell, Anne, 'Introduction', in Anne Lovell, Sefania Pandolfo, Veena Das and Sandra Laugier, *Face aux désastres. Conversation à quatre voix autour du care, la folie et les grandes détresses collectives* (Paris: Ithaque, 2013).

Lukács, Georg, *History and Class Consciousness: Studies in Marxist Dialectics*, trans. Rodney Livingstone (Cambridge, MA: The MIT Press, 1972).

Marcuse, Herbert, 'On Hedonism', *Negations*, trans. Jeremy J. Shapiro (London: MayFlyBooks, 2009), pp. 119–50.

Méda, Dominique, 'Pourquoi et comment mettre en œuvre un modèle à "deux apporteurs de revenus/deux pourvoyeurs de soins"?' *Revue Française de Socio-Économie*, 2 (2008), pp. 119–39.

Menke, Christoph, 'Tugend und Reflexion. Die Antinomie der Moralphilosophie', in Axel Honneth (ed.), *Dialektik der Freiheit. Frankfurter Adorno Konferenz 2003* (Frankfurt: Suhrkamp, 2005), pp. 142–62.

Molinier, Pascale, *Le Travail du care* (Paris: La Dispute, 2013).

Molinier, Pascale, Laugier, Sandra and Paperman, Patricia, 'Introduction', in Pascale Molinier, Sandra Laugier and Patricia Paperman (eds), *Qu'est-ce que le care?* (Paris: Payot, 2010), pp. 7–31.

Moutot, Gilles, *Essai sur Adorno* (Paris: Payot, 2010).

Noddings, Nel, *Caring: A Relational Approach to Ethics and Moral Education* (Berkeley: University of California Press, 1984).

Oksala, Johanna, 'Affective Labor and Feminist Politics', *Signs: Journal of Women in Culture and Society*, 41:2 (2016), pp. 281–303.

Pailhe, Ariane and Solaz, Anne, *Entre famille et travail, des arrangements de couples aux pratiques des employeurs* (Paris: La Découverte, 2009).

Paperman, Patricia, *Care et sentiments* (Paris: Presses universitaires de France, 2013).

Paperman, Patricia, 'Les gens vulnérables n'ont rien d'extraordinaire', in Patricia Paperman and Sandra Laugier (eds), *Le Souci des autres. Éthique et politique du care* (Paris: Éditions de l'EHESS, 2006).

Paperman, Patricia, 'Perspectives féministes sur la justice', *L'Année sociologique*, 54:2 (2004), pp. 413–33.

Paperman, Patricia and Molinier, Pascale (eds), *Contre l'indifférence des privilégiés. À quoi sert le care?* (Paris: Payot, 2013).

Parreñas, Rhacel, *Servants of Globalization: Women, Migration and Domestic Work* (Stanford: Stanford University Press, 2001).

Plumwood, Val, 'Nature, Self and Gender: Feminism, Environmental Philosophy, and the Critique of Rationalism', *Hypatia*, 6:1 (1991), pp. 3–27.

Raïd, Layla, 'De la *land ethic* aux éthiques du care', in Sandra Laugier (ed.), *Tous vulnérables?* (Petite Bibliothèque Payot, 2012), pp. 173–204.

Rosa, Hartmut, *Social Acceleration: A New Theory of Modernity*, trans. Jonathan Trejo-Mathys (New York: Columbia University Press, 2013).

Seel, Martin, 'Anerkennende Erkenntnis. Eine normative Theorie des Gebrauchs von Begriffen', *Adornos Philosophie der Kontemplation* (Frankfurt: Suhrkamp, 2004), pp. 42–63.

Shang, Jingzhi and Peloza, John, 'Can Real Men Consume Ethically? How Ethical Consumption Leads to Unintended Observer Inferences', *Journal of Business Ethics*, March 2015, pp. 1–17.

Sohn-Rethel, Alfred, *La Pensée-marchandise* (Bellecombe-en-Bauge: Éditions du Croquant, 2010).

Tronto, Joan, 'Beyond Gender Differences to a Theory of Care', *Signs*, 12:4 (1987), pp. 644–62.

Tronto, Joan, *Moral Boundaries: A Political Argument for an Ethic of Care* (New York: Routledge, 1993).

Van Nistelrooij, Inge, 'Self-sacrifice and Self-affirmation within Care-giving', *Medecine, Health Care and Philosophy*, 17:4 (2014), pp. 519–28.

Warren, Karen J., 'The Power and Promise of Ecological Feminism', in M. Zimmerman (ed.), *Environmental Philosophy: From Animal Rights to Radical Ecology* (Upper Saddle River, NJ: Prentice Hall, 1998), pp. 325–45.

Wiser, Antonin, 'Le tact, expérience de la littérature ou Proust lu par Adorno', *Philosophie*, 113 (2012), pp. 79–93.

Žižek, Slavoj, *The Ticklish Subject: The Absent Centre of Political Ontology* (London: Verso, 2000).

Index

9 781474 467407